# RAID ON

■

# QADDAFI

# RAID ON QADDAFI

THE UNTOLD STORY OF HISTORY'S

■

LONGEST FIGHTER MISSION BY

■

THE PILOT WHO DIRECTED IT

## COL. ROBERT E. VENKUS

ST. MARTIN'S PRESS

NEW YORK

Editor: Jared Kieling
Production Editor: Mark H. Berkowitz
Copyeditor: Olga Gardner
Design by Judith A. Stagnitto

Library of Congress Cataloging-in-Publication Data

Venkus, Robert.
    Raid on Qaddafi : the untold story of history's longest fighter mission by the pilot who directed it / Robert Venkus.
        p. cm.
    ISBN 0-312-07073-X
    1. Libya—History—Bombardment, 1986—Personal narratives, American. 2. Venkus, Robert. 3. Qaddafi, Muammar. I. Title.
E183.8.L75V46   1992
961.204'2—dc20                                                            91-33392
                                                                              CIP

First Edition: April 1992

10 9 8 7 6 5 4 3 2 1

Books are available in quantity for promotional or premium use.
Write to Director of Special Sales, St. Martin's Press, 175 Fifth Avenue, New York, N.Y. 10010, for information on discounts and terms, or call toll-free (800) 221-7945. In New York, call (212) 674-5151.

**TO THOSE WHO FLEW THE MISSION**

■

Operation El Dorado Canyon, April 14–15, 1986

# CONTENTS

■

## PREFACE

■

This is a true story of the United States Air Force raid on Tripoli, Libya, conducted during the night of April 14–15, 1986. It is not *the* true story of the mission; it is just one of many true stories, most of which will never be told, that came out of this unique feat of aerial combat. In these pages, the reader will share an insider's view of the events and decisions that led up to the raid, gain additional perspective on its execution, and learn more about its political and military effects as well as some of the controversy that still surrounds it.

The motivation to write this book sprang from several sources. It was born in the hours that followed Operation El Dorado Canyon, the code name of the total joint Air Force–Navy operation conducted against Libya that night. It grew in the period of mourning for the 48th Tactical Fighter Wing (TFW) crewmen who lost their lives. It was further nurtured by bitterness in the wake of events that followed the raid—events relating both to the author and especially to the 48th Wing and the men who flew the mission.

But this book might not have been written were it not for an incident that occurred almost eighteen months after the bombing. On a warm September weekday in 1987, I drove toward Washington, D.C., along the Baltimore-Washington parkway en route to that year's annual Air Force Association convention. Riding with me was an old friend who had retired from the service four years earlier. Our conversation was diverting, but not to the extent that I could forget my discomfort and nervousness. For the first time in my life, I would be attending a military function not as a uniformed officer of the U.S. Air Force, but as a civilian engineer representing a major defense contractor. My suit and tie felt just as strange as the small stack of business cards in my wallet. My friend recognized my edginess and attempted to distract me by steering the conversation to something more familiar. Not surprisingly, my role in the bombing of Libya came up.

"Is it true that you had a difficult time finding enough crews willing to fly the mission?" At first, I thought I had misunderstood his question. "Where in the world did you hear that?" I asked in shock. His admission that he had heard the same rumor both in industry and in the active Air Force stunned me just as much as his original query. The implications for those who flew the mission, and especially for those at RAF Lakenheath who had not, were highly disturbing. I suddenly realized that the dearth of accurate information about the raid that I had perceived over the past year was not just a product of my imagination. The lack of facts about what had happened in the 48th TFW before, during, and after the raid had created a vacuum—a vacuum which the grapevine had promptly filled with rumors. The fact that those rumors were now implying incompetence, shirking, and even cowardice was an insult to all of those involved in accomplishing one of the most unique missions in the history of military aviation. My mind was no longer on my ill-fitting, button-down collar. As I drove, a determination to set the record straight took hold. This book is a result of that determination.

This brief volume is not a disinterested history of the 48th Wing or of Operation El Dorado Canyon. As the reader will quickly realize, the author remains too personally involved to set down a totally objective summary of events for either the unit or the mission. Instead, this book is a compilation of my recollections of those events; I hesitate to call it a memoir, although sections of it certainly meet that definition. My portrayals are necessarily subjective and may occasionally lack the accuracy that some future historian will ensure in his or her account. They are based on my own cryptic notes, on some extensive but not all-encompassing research, and on a series of written or verbal interviews with many of the principals involved in the mission, including several of the aircrewmen who flew it. Each of the incidents detailed in these pages, some of which are controversial, has been verified through interviews or "sanity checks" with others who were either present or directly involved. Where appropriate, I have given credit to those authors who have chronicled Operation El Dorado Canyon elsewhere with varying degrees of accuracy, and to the interviewed individuals who volunteered their unique personal insights and gave permission for their names to be used.

The reader will also notice that certain facts and figures are missing from this account. Unfortunately, a large body of details concerning the mission remains classified as this book goes to press. Most notably, the names of the aircrewmen who flew the mission are conspicuously absent—for obvious reasons. Until very recently, the only people who had ever been publicly identified with the Air Force portion of El Dorado Canyon are Maj. Gen. Sam W. Westbrook III and the author.[1] Perhaps that will change someday, especially in the wake of Operation Desert Storm against Iraq, but this story must honor the crews' anonymity. An unavoidable result of such a decision is that the aircrews, both as a group and as individuals, do not receive the credit they deserve within this volume. That is especially true of the four superb squadron commanders (of the 492d, 493d, 494th, and 495th Tactical Fighter Squadrons) who served as the heart of the F-111F El Dorado Canyon attack force. In their varied roles, including leading the mission in the air and their squadrons on the ground, each of them performed outstandingly. To them, and to the many deserving others not mentioned either by design or omission, I offer my sincere apologies.

As to other facts that cannot yet be included, it was tempting to wait for details to become available in unclassified channels so that the story can be told completely. However, the realization that comparable details of other, earlier military operations still remain classified many years after the event prompts this early effort. Besides, as indicated in various public forums where the author has spoken about the mission, the releasable information holds a great deal of fascination for both military aviation enthusiasts and the general public. That circumstance has undoubtedly been reinforced by the stunning success of U.S. airpower in Operation Desert Storm. The use of the F-111F as a key element of that air campaign further illustrates why certain operational details of Operation El Dorado Canyon cannot yet be revealed.

There are four reasons why I think the level of interest in the raid of April 14–15, 1986, has remained high. No one can dispute the following facts:

1. The raid was the longest fighter combat mission, in terms of both time and distance flown, in the history of military aviation.[2]

2. The raid was flown against the most technologically sophisticated air defenses faced by any air force up to that time.

3. The raid was the first major combat mission for U.S. Air Force fighter aircraft in over a decade.

4. Based on the number of unique circumstances that were prerequisites for the mission, it is unlikely that another similar mission will occur in the foreseeable future.

The reader will discover, perhaps for the first time, that the mission was successfully accomplished despite a number of major obstacles. Taken together, these problems, some circumstantial and some man-made, had the potential of turning the raid into a disaster. Only a lot of hard work, guts, and luck prevented that outcome.

The reader should also recall that the 1986 bombing of Libya occurred within a geopolitical context very different from that which exists in the world today. El Dorado Canyon was conducted by people who normally devoted their full attention to the very real threat posed by the Soviet Union and the Warsaw Pact. For forty years, the focus of every NATO peacetime training sortie and exercise had been defense against that formidable foe. That perspective existed before the raid and resumed immediately afterward—some of the planes that attacked Tripoli were placed back on alert to strike Warsaw Pact targets within hours of the mission. The coming benefits of glasnost and perestroika were just a few years ahead but still entirely hidden to even the most prescient among us.

It is important to note that Operation El Dorado Canyon was the product of the efforts of many other units and people besides

the 48th TFW and the men and women stationed at RAF Lakenheath. President Ronald Reagan's orders for the mission included
major combatant units of the United States Navy and the United
States Air Force stationed both overseas and in the continental
U.S. (CONUS). The Navy conducted flight operations from two
carriers, the *America* and the *Coral Sea*, against targets in eastern
Libya and simultaneously provided support to the Tripoli bombers by engaging the Libyan air defenses. The 66th Electronic
Combat Wing, with aircraft maintained by the 20th TFW, provided critical electronic warfare support over Tripoli in the form
of EF-111 Ravens; those crews suffered the same level of stress
in almost every respect as the Lakenheath-based attackers. And,
of course, the historic length of the mission would have been an
impossibility without the armada of KC-10 and KC-135 tankers
from several units that gave El Dorado Canyon its long reach;
the saga of the tanker crews and planes from the U.S. who joined
this force at the last minute is a story in itself.[3]

A comprehensive telling of those worthy stories is beyond the
scope of this book and the personal experience of its author. The
account in these pages is necessarily largely confined to actions
and events involving the 48th Wing at Lakenheath, with many
of the details documented by the author's direct observation.

This book includes some observations about my former service
and the officers under whom I served. These remarks have not
been added gratuitously, but instead were inserted when the true
story made their inclusion necessary. While some both in and
out of uniform will disagree, I write this account as a friend of
the U.S. Air Force, not as an enemy or a critic. During over
twenty-four years of active service, I found that I loved many
things about the Air Force—hopefully those long-term affections
will also be evident in this recollection. But I also observed some
of my service's blemishes. Their exposure to public view, while
potentially embarrassing, may allow them to be cured rather than
covered cosmetically. In any event, the reader will make the final
judgement as to the author's objectivity. The facts you will read
have been recorded as I saw them.

One such fact is that Operation El Dorado Canyon, despite
its unique aspects, will never be more than a footnote in American military history. It involved less than thirty minutes of actual

combat; it cost just two U.S. casualties; and, after a brief period of worldwide interest and attention, it faded from the memory of most Americans. In the five years since the raid, it has been a subject of recurring interest only to the extent that it might serve as a benchmark against which other military capabilities can be measured. Developmental and maturing aircraft systems like the B-2 Stealth bomber, the F-117 Stealth fighter, and the F-15E Strike Eagle have all adopted the standard attitude: "While it took eighteen F-111Fs to strike three targets at Tripoli in 1986, just two (eight, twelve) B-2s (F-117s, F-15Es)—circle one—could have accomplished the same mission." The tremendous scope and phenomenal success of airpower used against Iraq in 1991 will no doubt serve to further obscure Operation El Dorado Canyon. Operation Desert Storm will justifiably become the new measuring stick against which future military air operations will be evaluated. Yet, had the raid on Tripoli not occurred, it is possible that Operation Just Cause (the 1989 invasion of Panama) and Operation Desert Storm might have unfolded quite differently. Perhaps neither of these operations would have been quite so brief and successful without the confident reliance on land-based precision bombing for which El Dorado Canyon set the stage.

It should also be noted that Operation Desert Storm has attested to the fact that the United States Air Force has very little dirty, or even slightly soiled, laundry to hide. Nevertheless, the fact that this book contains revelations of institutional problems and individual failures within the service will not find favor in the Pentagon, except perhaps near a fabled purple water fountain. Its reception in those quarters is insignificant when compared to its acceptance by the men and women who served in the 48th TFW, the Statue of Liberty Wing, in 1986. I feel confident that the people who made the mission happen will understand and accept this attempt to tell their story.

# ACKNOWLEDGMENTS

■

My greatest thanks go to the pilots and weapons systems operators of the 48th Tactical Fighter Wing who flew this historic mission, many of whom volunteered the details that constitute the bulk of this tale. Over five years later, they remain anonymous to the world and to their fellow citizens, but their achievement will justifiably live on in the annals of military aviation.

Secondly, I am especially grateful to my friend and classmate, Maj. Gen. Sam W. Westbrook III, United States Air Force (Retired). Sam's leadership in 1986 made the Air Force portion of El Dorado Canyon a success. His willingness to provide critical perspective and to correct my faulty memory when appropriate made the telling of the mission's story possible. Of course, he has no responsibility for any of this volume's inevitable faults; the author assumes full credit in that department.

A list of the others who helped would be long if they could all be identified. However, many of those who consented to interviews have asked to remain anonymous. Among those willing to be identified, Col. Bob Pastusek comes immediately to mind as a provider of key details and memory-checker extraordinaire.

I would also be remiss if I did not acknowledge the interest shown in this story by other publishers which sustained the momentum toward completing the book. The encouragement and suggestions provided by Peder Lund were instrumental in that regard. Of course, Peder's decision to steer the author to literary agent Ethan Ellenberg proved to be the biggest step in turning the idea into a reality. Ethan's sage advice on style and content are incorporated throughout this volume, albeit with limited success by this neophyte writer.

Finally, not just because it is traditional but because it is true, the author's family deserves a large measure of credit for permitting this long-term project to finally bear fruit. Joyce and our four children were always loving, always there, supportive when support was needed, and inspirational when inspiration was below "bingo." (See Glossary.)

Without the cooperation and support of all these people, this book would not have been possible. If a single sentence in this volume prompts one positive change within the United States Air Force; or if some future contingency mission somehow benefits from this account, I will consider this effort a success.

# RAID ON

■

# QADDAFI

# TAKEOFF

At precisely 17:36 Greenwich mean time, April 14, 1986, Lieutenant Colonel F., the pilot of the first of twenty-four F-111Fs, released brakes on RAF Lakenheath's Runway 24. His forty-five-ton General Dynamics fighter bomber began to rapidly accelerate, pushed along smartly by the thrust of two Pratt & Whitney TF-30P-100 afterburning turbofan engines. Despite the extra weight of twelve Mark-82 five-hundred-pound bombs, the aircraft reached takeoff speed within twenty seconds. As it lifted into the evening skies of Suffolk, England, it marked a historic moment for the United States Air Force: the first major USAF combat mission in the war against terrorism was underway.

Behind the lead aircraft, forty-six other pilots and weapons systems operators (commonly called WSOs, pronounced "Whizohs," for short) prepared to take off at precise intervals in order to join with their refueling tankers. Their F-111Fs looked ungainly and downright ugly in go-to-war camouflage paint, loaded down with tons of ordnance and with wings that looked broken and disjointed in their high-lift, takeoff configuration. But the crews were not worried about cosmetics at the moment: over ninety percent of them were beginning what would be their first combat mission. Many were just coming to the realization that they were really going and that this was not just another show of force. And, considering the improbable set of circumstances under which the mission was being launched, it was not surprising that some still harbored doubts as they rolled down the runway. Over fourteen hours later, they hoped, they would be completing a record-setting flight: the longest fighter combat mission in terms of both time and distance in the history of military aviation. But as dusk settled over their home base at Lakenheath, making history was the least of their concerns. None of them were certain that they would reach Libya: six spares were being launched to ensure that eighteen of the twenty-four would go on to the three targets in and around Tripoli. During the next ninety minutes, each plane would be checked and double checked, and only eighteen "good jets" would continue on the mission. The other six would return to Suffolk, some with bitterly disappointed crews who would forever curse their bad luck that April night.

As he retracted the landing gear and began to climb, Lieutenant Colonel F.'s thoughts flashed back to his first combat mission in the Aardvark more than fourteen years earlier over Vietnam. The anticipation then had not been much worse than it was now; in both cases, the fear of facing the unknown was overriden by the demands of hundreds of mental and physical tasks needed to get the job done. But in 1972, an underlying question had required an answer: could the airplane do the job?

Recognition for the F-111 had been late arriving. In 1968, the first F-111s were sent to combat in Southeast Asia prematurely, and they promptly killed some of the best crews in the Air Force. The plane's single-ship night mission also meant that most of these losses were mysterious and difficult to explain. A jet would launch into the pitch-black Thai night, refuel and depart its jet tanker en route to a target in North Vietnam, and then disappear.

Some wrecks were eventually found, and plausible explanations were postulated for each crash. Withdrawn from the war as quickly as it had been sent, the F-111 would return in 1972 to perform respectably in a role acknowledged by all to be very difficult and dangerous. But the Aardvark's reputation had been sullied forever—half of the six F-111s deployed to Thailand in 1968 had been lost in less than a month. As an F-105 Thud driver at the time, I vividly recall the F-111's reputation as a "Widow

Maker." Despite our own airplane's recognized hazards—the Thud had had its share of problems—we "real" fighter pilots and our WSOs and EWOs (Electronic Warfare Officers) fought long, desperate battles with the personnel gurus to avoid being assigned to the Aardvark. More than one of my contemporaries left the service rather than accept the assignment.

Those who had ended up flying the F-111 developed a defensive attitude about their new calling. In the author's opinion, traces of that attitude can still be found in the F-111 community today. The one time it almost completely disappeared was after the historic raid on Libya.

Many of the crewmen who remained at Lakenheath after the mission's takeoff had sensed that this might indeed be a chance of a lifetime. Major S., another veteran of combat in Southeast Asia, had found out just how much that chance meant to one of his fellow fighter jocks. Carrying both the Buddha and the St. Christopher medal which had served him so well fourteen years earlier, Major S. had been preparing to leave the squadron for his aircraft that afternoon. Suddenly a young captain had approached him and shoved a crisp one-hundred-dollar bill into his hand. "I've got nine more of these if you will let me take your place on the raid," he offered. Major S. smiled in surprise, and told the captain that he did not own enough money to get on the mission. The disappointed junior pilot was one of many crewmen in the 48th Tactical Fighter Wing (TFW) who would have done almost anything to fly in combat that night. They thought they would retire from the military without ever getting another chance; perhaps many will. Some, but not all, have since seen combat over Iraq and Kuwait.

Takeoff is normally a routine phase of flight, although aircrews are extremely alert to possible critical problems during the few seconds that separate taxiing from flying. It is considered "routine" because it is done using normal radio communications and typically involves launching and joining into formation no more than four aircraft. In comparison, the launch of Operation El Dorado Canyon was highly complex, with a simple but difficult-to-achieve goal: get almost sixty fighters and tankers airborne from four different bases, and do it in such a manner that not everyone in England knows that a major combat mission is underway. To accomplish this, the fighters would launch "Comm Out," in total radio silence. They would silently join on their respective tankers, who would perform all necessary communications with the British ground controllers. The fighters would fly tight formation with the tankers, and turn off their electronic identification equipment known as IFF, "Identification Friend or Foe," so that on radar the raiding party would appear to be just an unarmed formation of air refueling tankers.

That seemingly harmless force was en route to a point beyond Land's End, the southwestern tip of England, where it would leave the structured system of air traffic control and continue "With Due Regard." That innocuous phrase from the international flight manuals allows any plane of any nation to fly in international airspace without monitoring or control from outside agencies. In effect, it allows you to go anywhere and do almost anything on your own responsibility. El Dorado Canyon's raiding force was utilizing this flexible feature of the international flight rules to effectively hide itself and its intentions once it got beyond British airspace.

The "Comm Out" launch of the mission almost had immediate disastrous results. First, a last-minute runway change due to a wind shift at Mildenhall meant that the heavy tankers would be taking off to the north rather than to the south. No change was necessary at Lakenheath, however, and by the time the tankers' intentions were known, none was possible. Precise procedures and timing data had been practiced for use in all weather conditions, but at the last minute the three flight leaders noticed that they were unlikely to work due to the unexpected winds and tanker changes. Backup plans using electronic equipment and the old, dependable eyeball were discussed but no decision was made. In the end, the critical process of joining with the tankers immediately after takeoff was done to a great extent using what fighter pilots call TLAR: "That Looks About Right."

Second, within minutes of the takeoff, the irate commander of a nearby Royal Air Force base called RAF Lakenheath demanded to speak to the commanding officer. Was I aware, he asked, that a large formation of U.S. aircraft had just passed perilously close to a line of Tornado fighters recovering at his base? I apologized for the incursion, replying that our normal coordination procedures had apparently broken down and that I would ensure that it would not happen again. In fact, the near mid-air collision had occurred because our U.S. jets had not contacted the appropriate controlling agency for the airspace they flew through. This problem was also caused by the runway change, and its consequences were nearly catastrophic. Only good fortune and alert USAF and RAF aircrews prevented that result.

Eventually, just thirty-six crewmen, including Lieutenant Colonel F. and Major S., would continue on their way to Libya. These men all shared a major, nagging uncertainty: would they be coming home the next morning? The demands of the initial air refuelings and their systems checks (attack radar, terrain-following radar, inertial navigators, etc.) would repeatedly distract them from this concern, but would never completely remove it. On a mission of this length, there would be moments when thoughts one would prefer to ignore—including thoughts of dying—could not be ignored. Air Force intelligence officers had reassuringly briefed them that the Libyan air defenders normally shut down and went to bed after midnight. But the crews who were streaking toward the Mediterranean had every reason to be worried. Without a doubt, the Libyans knew they were coming.

**MARCH 1985**

**LAKENHEATH AND THE F-111**

RAF Lakenheath was beset by typically dismal weather as my family and I arrived there in March of 1985. The same chilly, damp, overcast weather pattern would persist throughout the upcoming year. It became so repetitious that one season blended into the next—you could not tell the difference without consulting a calendar. But the weather was not about to get us down: we were beginning a much anticipated assignment to the 48th Tactical Fighter Wing where I would serve as the vice wing commander.

The 48th TFW had recently celebrated its twenty-fifth anniversary in England. Arriving in F-100 Super Sabres in 1960, the wing had changed aircraft three times since moving to Suffolk. The final upgrade had occurred in 1977 when the wing became the only unit in the U.S. Air Force to be equipped with F-111Fs.

The 48th's history dated back to World War II and included several years in France after the war's end. Stationed at Chaumont Air Base, close to the site where the Statue of Liberty had been designed, the wing was officially named the "Statue of Liberty Wing" in 1954. The Chaumont villagers had asked for the designation, feeling that the wing represented all Americans who had died in France during both World Wars. The 48th was and is the only United States Air Force unit with both an official name and number.

I realized that serving as second-in-command of a major line combat unit was going to be both a privilege and a challenge. But I expected that it was also going to be a lot of fun. I would be flying fighters again, and working for an Air Force Academy classmate and friend of twenty-six years, Col. Sam W. Westbrook III. The icing on the cake would be provided by the intangible rewards gained from being as close to the front lines as any full colonel can get in the U.S. Air Force. The tactical combat "tooth" of the Air Force is made up of less than thirty-five combat wings of fighter and attack aircraft worldwide. The wings based in Europe were within striking range of the Warsaw Pact armies and air forces which, in 1986, seemed likely to be their primary targets in a European war. As a result, the 48th "Statue of Liberty" Wing was prepared at all times to fly and fight from its cozy home near the village of Lakenheath in the region known as East Anglia. With only four colonels in each of those far-flung wings actively flying, I considered myself lucky to be among the few senior officers still practicing the trade of a combat-ready fighter pilot.

My initial checkout in the earlier model F-111A had occurred early in 1985. Leaving my family in Germany, I traveled to Mountain Home Air Force Base in Idaho to begin my acquaintance with the plane its crews call the "Aardvark" or "Switchblade." The Air Force usually gives official names to its aircraft (the F-111 has none), but aircrews inevitably settle on their own unofficial versions, which are generally less reverent and more descriptive. "Aardvark" refers to the F-111's long nose and ungainly posture on the ground, while "Switchblade" perfectly describes the jet's primary design feature: variable swept wings. Those wings, selectively positioned at sweep angles from sixteen to seventy-two degrees, allow the F-111 to reconfigure itself in flight. The F-111 was the first operational combat aircraft in the world to have this capability.

The airplane's unique operational characteristics were something I looked forward to with a mixture of curiosity and anticipation. The F-111 was, and is, the Air Force's primary night interdiction aircraft, used to attack critical targets deep in enemy territory around the clock. To better perform this role, it uses an automatic terrain-following system based on early 1960's technology. My short "executive" checkout in the "Vark" included both day and night missions using the system, with the night sorties (a single flight of a single aircraft) proving especially interesting. Thoughts of celebrating my upcoming forty-fourth birthday kept me highly motivated as I learned the intricacies of trusting your life to a sophisticated bank of redundant computers at low altitude in the dark. I eventually became as comfortable with the Terrain-Following (TF) system as anyone could in eighteen months—not very. The fact is that the experienced crews who fly, and thrive, on this mission become so knowledgeable about the TF's workings that they become a key part of its fail safe features. And, as happened on my first night, in-the-weather, automatic-terrain-following mission, their knowledge often proves to be the last resort that ensures survival.

After twenty minutes of perfect operation through the mountains of Idaho's Snake River valley, the TF system suffered a subtle failure that gave us (my instructor pilot and me) no indication that a potentially fatal descent command had been issued. The computers dutifully followed orders, and we started a gradual dive toward the invisible "granite overcast"[1] ahead. Armed with two weeks of academic cramming and a well-developed survival instinct, I detected the problem at the same instant as the instructor, disengaged the auto pilot, and climbed manually to a safe recovery. That experience gave me healthy respect for the F-111's TF capabilities—and limitations! After arriving at Lakenheath, I tried to establish rapport with the flyers at the first wing flying safety meeting I attended. Introduced by Sam Westbrook and asked to say a few words, I referred to the low-level, automatic-terrain-following aspect of their mission—an aspect of flying viewed with undisguised loathing (and a touch of fear) by even the hottest F-16 or F-15 "Top Gun." My admission that night automatic TF-ing was "the first unnatural act I ever performed that I didn't enjoy" drew raucous cheers of approval from the Switchblade drivers and their WSOs.

The quick checkout in the arctic conditions of Idaho was followed by a return trip to Germany to tie up loose ends. With all in order for the move, my family and I departed Ramstein village on March 7, 1985, arriving in England that night after a full day of driving and ferrying.

At Lakenheath, we quickly discovered that we were joining a smoothly functioning, combat-oriented unit that, while similar to every other fighter wing I had known, was also uniquely different. Part of that difference was based on the aircraft the wing flies. The 48th was the only USAF wing equipped with the F-111F. Unlike other models of the F-111, the "F" had certain distinct avionics systems and one-of-a-kind jet engines that provide great performance advantages. The TF-30P-100, Pratt and Whitney engines, produced almost fifty percent more thrust than similar engines on other F-111s, but they also experienced a much higher failure rate. Those engine failures contributed to an overall "break rate" on the wing's aircraft that in 1985 was among the highest in the Air Force. Roughly forty percent of returning sorties would suffer some failure that required a maintenance fix before the aircraft could be flown again.

The typical F-111F training sortie was also different. Lasting well over two hours, it required a new perspective and careful planning of coffee intake for someone like me: over a span of twenty-two years, I had acquired a well-trained "1.5-hour butt." A longer sortie allowed the accomplishment of a lot more training than in most other jets. However, when coupled with the break rate mentioned earlier, it also meant that each "F" model produced many fewer sorties than most other fighters. Checking the Air Force management measure of sorties-per-aircraft-per-month, the F-111F produced an average of fewer than eleven, while the newer General Dynamics fighter, the F-16, yielded over twenty. These figures translated into a very small number of flights per month for each of the wing's aircrews. It was also the reason why I would only fly once or twice each week. If we colonels took more sorties, the inexperienced lieutenants in the squadrons would get even fewer than the ten or eleven flights they were scrambling for each month. The Aardvark always put a premium on training time for aircrews, an important consideration when it came to practicing the wing's most common, and most hazardous, mission.

The F-111's primary mission was and is precision attack of enemy targets in all weather conditions and at night. The all-weather and night aspects of the job make the F-111 different from most other aircraft, and indispensable to the planners of tactical air campaigns. Doctrine calls for airpower to keep pressure on an enemy both day and night. The problem is how to strike targets around the clock, and in 1986 the F-111's blind bombing capability provided the only answer for tactical planners. As a result, the Switchblade has always played a more important role in Air Force planning than its small numbers (less than 360 remain flying) would seem to justify. Reluctantly, the Air Force agreed that "McNamara's Folly,"[2] the plane that was supposed to do everything for everybody, and which the Navy then cleverly avoided buying, had gradually evolved into a combat aircraft which outperformed all other fighter and attack aircraft in its particular role. Even the Air Force's new F-15E and advanced versions of the Navy's A-6 are, at best, only marginally more effective in bombing than their twenty-year-old F-111 cousins, but they still do not possess all of the Aardvark's all-weather capability. New technologies built into the F-15E Strike Eagle and the A-6 Intruder make some of their individual systems more useable and effective than those on the Aardvark. But, when comparing overall effectiveness in the surface attack role, many would agree with my contention that the F-111 is still the winner. As a matter of interest, the F-117 Stealth Fighter is not all-weather, and has both a smaller weapons-carrying capacity and less range than the F-111.

In comparison to other F-111s, the F-111F's ability to perform the deep interdiction mission at night was greatly improved by a system called "Pave Tack."[3] Built by what was then Ford Aerospace, the Pave Tack pod is carried in the F-111's internal bomb bay on a rotating cradle. The pod contains a sophisticated, precise targeting system for around-the-clock weapons deliveries even in marginal weather. Utilizing both a Forward-Looking InfraRed (FLIR) camera and a Laser Designator, Pave Tack allows the F-111F to see its target in the dark or through some obscurations such as fog, mist, and light smoke. It then permits delivery of Laser Guided Bombs (LGBs) precisely on target by beaming laser energy directly at the aim point until bomb impact.

LGBs are World War II–style "dumb" bombs turned "smart" by laser guidance modification kits. They fall ballistically until they see a laser beam reflecting from their target, and then they guide to it using maneuverable control fins during their last few seconds of flight. These bombs had proven their worth during the war in Southeast Asia. Some difficult, well-defended targets had withstood multiple strikes by many aircraft with dumb bombs. Those attacks had produced minimal damage while costing us many crews and planes. The targets were ultimately destroyed by a few jets using LGBs. In 1986, various LGBs were still the bread-and-butter precision munition in our inventory at Lakenheath, despite promise of very expensive developmental systems to provide greater standoff capability. "Standoff" is the distance between the target and the aircraft attacking it—ideally, that distance is long in order to prevent multimillion-dollar jets from coming within range of cheap but effective anti-aircraft artillery, also known as "Triple-A" or flak. Unfortunately, effective affordable precision munitions with significant standoff capability have proven very difficult to develop. They can be built, but not cheaply. They will almost inevitably turn out to be too expensive to buy, except in small quantities. Accordingly, in my opinion these munitions have been, are now, and will always be the hope of the future.

The Air Force of 1986 planned on the vast majority of its tactical sorties flying to within a few thousand yards of their targets. That was certainly the case in the F-111F, where even the best "Pave Tack Toss" maneuver placed the jet within two miles of the aim point for its weapons. The practice needed to safely and effectively perform this maneuver at night was the driving factor in the wing's training program. Without a lot of practice, many of the LGBs would miss their targets. The dangers and complexities of this weapons delivery technique will become dramatically clear as the details of the night raid on Tripoli are presented.

# TWO

# DEPARTURE

C aptain N. felt like he was tiptoeing through a minefield. As WSO of the lead aircraft going to the Tripoli airport, he had taken off first and would eventually land last—fourteen hours later. But at the moment he shared the feelings of each of the other twenty-three right-seaters as they checked out all their various systems during departure. Every time Captain N. threw a switch or pushed a button, he knew that his action could result in an abort for him and his pilot. His single chance to fly in combat after seven years of training could disappear in a momentary blink of a warning light or the steady display of an improper value on some crucial gauge.

With the raid governed by stringent Rules of Engagement (ROE), no F-111F would be going to Libya unless all of the systems needed to deliver its bombs accurately were fully functional. The three targets at Tripoli were all militarily significant, with documented roles in the training or organization of the Libyan military or terrorist groups. In addition, the Air Force had gone to great lengths to ensure against "collateral damage," the well-understood euphemism for the killing or maiming of innocent civilians. Captain N. knew that the combat veteran sitting to his left would have to bite the bullet and abort if the attack radar, or the Inertial Navigation System, or the see-in-the-dark Pave Tack pod failed during these initial airborne checks. And, because of the route they were flying to their target, they also needed a fully operational terrain-following radar. Checking each of these systems, none of which were known for being overly reliable, was a nerve-wracking task. In the gathering dark, Captain N. breathed a bit easier as each of them in turn passed its respective tests. Now, he thought, if his pilot and the tanker's boom operator could just keep from damaging the air refueling system, this particular F-111 would not have to turn back.

As Land's End, the southwesternmost tip of England, faded into the gathering darkness, twelve of Captain N.'s buddies in six other F-111Fs were not so lucky. They banked sharply, turning northbound to Lakenheath; some because they were designated spares who were not needed, others because their jets could not meet the tough ROE. None of the twelve were happy to be going home so soon—they had come too far to want to return without having proven themselves in combat. And they were now absolutely certain that their squadron mates were about to do just that.

Major S. also vividly recalls the scene as the El Dorado Canyon task force passed Land's End. The sunset was beautiful, casting a reddish tinge on the small cumulus clouds below. But it was not as impressive as the huge aerial armada on its way to Libya. On his single-ship combat sorties in Southeast Asia, he had never been part of a big package, sometimes known as a "Gorilla." Now, everywhere he looked, the sky was full of airplanes: KC-135s refueling KC-10s; KC-10s refueling F-111s and EF-111s, the latter glowing pink as their gray paint reflected the sunset. Almost sixty jets stretched across the darkening skies. It was awesome: as another pilot, Captain J., commented after the raid in an oblique reference to a famous movie scene, "You could just hear 'The Ride of the Valkyries!'"

Even if some of the crewmen remained skeptical until well into the mission, some of their wives had not doubted that their husbands were going to war. A few crewmen actually told their wives they were about to fly a combat mission; others could not hide actions that were outright tip-offs to their spouses. On Sunday when Major S. had searched a dresser for his tiny good-luck Buddha, his wife had not missed the clue. At breakfast on Monday, the day of the raid, she served him coffee in a cup from his Southeast Asia combat squadron. On the other hand, some wives had no idea that their husbands were about to go into combat. One squadron commander's wife distinctly remembers her thoughts that day that worldwide peace seemed to be at hand. As her husband flew south to bomb Tripoli, she reveled in the idea that war seemed so unlikely. In another instance, a young woman, whose husband would also fly the mission, was several months pregnant and unaware of the impending mission. The wife of another crewman, correctly reading the tea leaves through frequent exposure to the BBC, decided to keep her pregnant neighbor in the dark.

Captain N. had been one of the more difficult crewmen to convince that the mission was really "a go." It had taken the presence of the Air Force's Chief of Staff Gen. Charles Gabriel at the previous night's briefing to convince him that the U.S. was really about to launch a strike against Libya. General Gabriel's low-key speech had proven to Captain N. that they would, indeed, be going. But it had not succeeded in putting him in the right frame of mind for the mission. When he awoke on Monday, April 14, he took advantage of his wife's absence to switch his VCR on and watch a "Rambo" movie. In retrospect, he believes it had the desired effect. Captain N. was keyed up with a full load of adrenaline as he headed south paralleling the French coast. He would retain that attitude despite the grueling marathon of a mission he was flying. As a matter of interest, his pilot, Lieutenant Colonel F., was even more skeptical about the mission really being on. It wasn't until they had departed the tanker south of Sicily and begun diving and accelerating toward the Mediterranean that he accepted that they were really going to bomb Libya. Until then, he thought that the whole mission could be nothing more than a spectacular show of force.

But that point in the mission was still hours away and other problems had to be solved in the meantime. The first one was the delicate business of night air refueling.

**APRIL 1985**

**FERNANDO'S ACCIDENT**

My first few months in the 48th TFW were relatively uneventful. Flying in European conditions, especially the awful English weather, proved challenging for an aging colonel experiencing it for the first time. But, despite low overcasts and limited visibilities, I enjoyed every minute of flying time—two and a half years at a desk had been much too long! Only one minor incident marred the spring of 1985. While it was indeed a minor incident, it could very well have been a fatal disaster. And, prophetically, it would happen while Colonel Westbrook was away and I was the acting wing commander.

The U.S. service academies provide highly ordered environments based on a whole series of rules and regulations. None of these is more immutable than alphabetical order. Based on its imperatives, Sam Westbrook and I had stood in adjoining ranks on June 26, 1959, our first day at the Air Force Academy in Colorado. While friends, we had not become very close during the remainder of our four years there. Sam had earned early recognition as an outstanding academician and military cadet. Meanwhile, I had plodded along as one of the "great unwashed middle" of the class of '63. Over twenty-five years later, I had joined his wing as second in command. Working for a friend and classmate can be a sensitive, difficult situation, but it turned out to be a very pleasant, rewarding experience for me.

Sam and I had taken very different routes to the headquarters of the 48th TFW. After serving as the cadet wing commander at the Academy, Sam had graduated first in our class of almost 500. He had accepted his diploma from President John F. Kennedy on that glorious June day in Colorado, and had departed immediately to pursue an advanced degree at Oxford as a Rhodes Scholar. Three years spent there earned him a bachelor/master of arts honors degree, as well as a bachelor of science degree in plasma physics.

Sam Westbrook then went on to pilot training at the same base in Arizona where I had earned my wings three years earlier. After graduation in 1968, he was assigned to Nellis AFB near Las Vegas where he began his long relationship with the F-111. He flew the F-111 into 1971, serving with distinction as a fighter pilot and weapons and tactics officer. While there, he began his string of well-earned early promotions when he was selected "below the zone" for advancement from captain to major. Back then, the Air Force used potential as the primary criteria for promotion—on-the-job performance was considered secondary. Unfortunately for many, this priority was not reversed until the late 1980s. It did not matter in Sam's case: by either standard he was an undeniable standout. He volunteered for combat in Southeast Asia, and in 1972 began to earn his battle spurs flying the A-1E from Thailand. Returning to Nellis and the F-111, Sam became the chief of the operational testing section for the Aardvark in late 1973.

Sam's second tour at Nellis could have lasted three or more years, but his potential and performance dictated that he be given a chance to do a lot more than the average fighter jock. So in 1975 the new Lieutenant Colonel–selectee was assigned to the Pentagon as a staff action officer. During his almost five years in Washington, Sam's duties included nine months on the National Security Council staff in a position similar to that later held by Lt. Col. Oliver North, USMC; and a stint as chief of the staff group for the Assistant Vice Chief of Staff of the Air Force. Suitably initiated into the Pentagon's mysterious workings and long since promoted again to colonel, by 1980 Sam Westbrook was deemed ready for a return to the Air Force's front lines.

In July of that year, he took over as the deputy commander for operations of the F-111E wing at Upper Heyford near England's scenic Cotswolds. Two years of enjoyable flying there were followed by one year of grooming as director of inspection of the United States Air Forces in Europe (USAFE). Finally, Sam was assigned to Lakenheath and the 48th Wing as the vice wing commander in 1983. Fate assured his eventual rendezvous with Colonel Qaddafi when he assumed command of the wing in April 1984.

By the time I arrived as his vice commander in 1985, Sam was well established in a successful tour of duty in the most challenging job most Air Force officers can imagine. With over 5,000 people and eighty fighter bombers under his command, he controlled an investment of approximately three billion of the U.S. taxpayers' dollars. And he did it with the grace and good humor which typified his performance throughout his career. As described by Andrew Cockburn in a *Playboy* article on the raid, Sam was "ambitious but popular," a difficult combination to carry off under the best of circumstances.[1] He did it then and continued to do so until his retirement in 1991 as the major general in charge of all operations within the Air Force's Training Command.

As for me, I had gone straight to pilot training from the Academy, beginning a career as an operational flyer that, with only brief interruptions, would span the next twenty-four years. Four years as an instructor pilot in Oklahoma, teaching others to fly, were followed by five years as a fighter pilot in the biggest, prettiest single-seat fighter ever built, the F-105 Thunderchief. The "Thud" took me to war, and brought me back without a scratch, on 169 combat missions. It was not as kind to others, however—fifteen pilots checked out in our class in Kansas and five were dead within eighteen months. We had expected the war to be winding down when we arrived in Thailand in late 1969. We were proven wrong.

I flew the Thud on consecutive tours in Thailand, Okinawa, and Nevada, where my path crossed Sam's for the first time since our graduation. My last tour in the F-105 ended in 1974. After attending the Air Force's staff college, I was assigned as a liaison to the U.S. Army infantry school at Fort Benning, Georgia. Three years passed before I returned to flying fighters in California. During four years of flying F-4s, I served as operations officer of two squadrons, commanded a third, remarried (my first marriage had not survived the wilds of Georgia), lost half an inch of height ejecting from a burning F-4G, and was promoted early to colonel.

This last, unexpected event catapulted me into the ranks of the "fast burners" for the first time in my career. On the strength of the promotion and some successful staff leadership during my two years in Germany, in 1985 I found myself chosen to become Lakenheath's "lady in waiting." Both naive and ambitious, I began to think that promotion to flag rank was a possibility. This condition is known in the military as having "stars in your eyes." Given a strong foothold, it can readily cloud the most objective judgement and cause the reassessment of long-held views on honesty and integrity. In other words, officers can reach a state where they will consider doing almost anything in order to be promoted to general. Luckily the realities of the raid on Libya would prevent me from ever acquiring a full-blown case of this malady.

As indicated earlier, Sam Westbrook had been a "fast burner" from day one. But, despite his meteoric success, he had maintained strong ties with the real Air Force and the real people who make it fly. While Sam knew how to prevent political damage to his career, and to profit from an opportunity when it presented itself, he was not a "political animal." I once asked him how he managed to survive in the jungle of service politics without becoming one of "them." His answer was a classic: "You can't always prevent someone from stabbing you in the back; the trick is to identify the one who did it before he gets his hand off the knife, and then *never* let him do it again." I tried to absorb this and other lessons from a man who was demonstrably superior to most of the other commanders I had served and observed during my career. As time would prove, I had limited success in retaining all the knowledge that Sam had made available to me.

On April 16, 1985, the 48th TFW came very close to losing an airplane in an incident on our main runway. Colonel Westbrook had departed early in the afternoon to observe a continent-wide competition involving weapons loading specialists from each of the USAF fighter wings in Europe.[2] The 81st TFW was hosting the event at the RAF base at Bentwaters some forty-five miles east of Lakenheath. Later that afternoon, I chaired a regular staff meeting in our headquarters building located within yards of our main runway. The meeting came to an abrupt end when a loud explosion shook the building, stopping the briefing officer in his tracks. Before any of us could reach a door in the windowless room, the portable radios (commonly called "bricks") began to buzz with chatter about an F-111 having gone off the runway. As we raced away from the hurriedly canceled meeting, we could see the wreck of our jet sitting cockeyed in the distance. However, it would be several days before the full details of the accident would become clear.

As we learned later, the aircraft had been flying a mission to check out the terrain-following radars before that critical system could be used by regular line aircrews. The flight was required as part of a functional check flight, or FCF, a "test hop" by an experienced crew normally required after any major maintenance. After a low-level flight in Scotland to accomplish the checks, the crew began experiencing radio problems while at high altitude on the way back to England. That problem intensified, eventually cutting out all two-way communications with the ground. Things got worse when the pilot lowered the landing gear: one of the lights required to indicate "down-and-locked" wheels did not light up. The crew completed the appropriate checklist for the malfunction, got a green light from the tower at Lakenheath (the standard signal to a radioless aircraft for "cleared to land"), and proceeded to nurse their ailing Aardvark onto our main runway.

The landing seemed normal until about 5,000 feet down the runway when one of the two main landing gear tires exploded, which resulted in the concussion that shook the headquarters. The jet then veered toward the left side of the runway and the pilot, for reasons not immediately clear, was unable to keep it on the prepared runway surface. Within seconds, the extended landing gear reached the soft soil left of the runway, digging in, swinging the jet further left, and preventing any chance of recovery. As the F-111 slid to a stop, the gear struts collapsed toward the aircraft's tail, damaging the plane's belly and the gear doors.

The good news was that no one was injured and that the jet was salvageable—the pilot's decision not to eject had proven sound. We even hoped that the sensitive jet engines had not been too badly damaged by ingesting mud and debris. With no fuel leaking and the plane surrounded by fire trucks (on the scene in seconds from their positions on alert close by), it appeared that we were going to get away with what the Air Force calls a "Class B" accident—no one had died, the plane was repairable, and the dollar value of the damage appeared to be less than the prescribed limit.

Of course, all of this would remain true only if we could keep from further damaging the jet during removal from its position just off the runway. That prospect sounds easy enough until you envision thirty tons of fighter plane mired in the deep Suffolk mud. The task would be a long, tedious one involving lots of digging, fashioning jack supports, jacking the plane up, rigging support and guidelines, and finally hauling the jet away with "Big Bertha," our huge mobile crane. It made us all envious of the rumored Navy wartime (and sometimes peacetime!) mode of operation of just pushing any wreck smartly over the side of the carrier! If this had happened in combat, we would have done something not too different—bulldoze the plane aside—in order to reopen our closed runway for combat launches and recoveries.[3]

Colonel Westbrook returned in the early evening as I supervised the initial stages of the delicate salvage operation. Working under improvised portable lights, several hundred of the wing's maintenance people labored to free the stuck jet, taking great care not to hurt it in the process. It was well after midnight when our balky "Big Bertha" finally did her thing and lifted the F-111F out of the dirt—while dozens of us clung to guide ropes to keep the jet from swinging or tilting dangerously. A long, careful walk followed as the dangling Aardvark, with guide ropes held taut by a tired but satisfied group of Statue of Liberty Wing members, was finessed into a waiting hangar. The field reopened for business the next morning as though nothing bad had happened. But, from the command section's point of view, that was not exactly true.

Performing a maneuver common to every flight, although under slightly unusual circumstances, one of our aircraft had come uncomfortably close to being totally destroyed. While still traveling fast enough to do considerable damage to itself, it had passed within ten feet of a concrete barrier stanchion that housed the cable which crosses the runway to catch the tailhook of a plane experiencing an emergency. If the F-111 had slid across this formidable, immovable obstacle, its guts would have been ripped out, spilling flammable jet fuel and hydraulic fluid, probably causing a catastrophic explosion and fire. The crew would have had to be very quick and very lucky to survive.

The seriousness of the accident made Sam and me determined to find out exactly how and why it had occurred. Colonel Westbrook ordered that the incident be investigated at the local level as if it had been a major accident. The wide-ranging investigation that ensued inevitably focused on the actions of the crew in responding to the blown tire. Why had they been unable to keep the plane on the runway?

If the pilot had used all of the resources available to him, he should have been able to keep his jet on the friendly surface provided by the concrete and asphalt runway. As his speed decreased and the controls lost effectiveness, he still had his functioning brake and, more importantly, his nosewheel steering system to help him guide a more or less straight course. Using the nosewheel steering should have counteracted the effects of the blown tire and the skidding wheel, allowing the plane to be stopped on the runway with only minor damage.

Unfortunately, the pilot had forgotten to use nosewheel steering. His explanation was an honest admittance that, in the few seconds available to him, he had failed to recall an emergency procedure on which he had drilled dozens of times.

But Sam and I did not read too much into this single error. There had been some continuing emphasis on the use of nosewheel steering within the wing, but our crews retained some residual distrust of a system which could be dangerous itself, as much of their training had stressed. They all knew that a hard-over nosewheel malfunction can take a plane off a runway or taxiway faster than any other problem. As a result, the campaign to encourage the system's use had had limited success with all of our pilots.

Another more important reason not to overreact to the pilot's mistake was that the particular pilot involved was one of our best—a select member of the wing's "Stan Eval" (Standardization and Evaluation) section, chosen to fly with and evaluate all the wing's crewmen. As one of our "Stanley Evils" (crew slang for these respected but occasionally feared evaluators), Capt. Fernando Ribas-Dominicci was capable of taking the inevitable ribbing, and was unlikely to repeat his mistake. Our faith in Fernando proved well placed—he performed superbly from that point until the night he died on his first combat mission. And, as events would prove, it took both a faulty tactical plan and fully alerted defenses to bring him down near Tripoli, Libya, almost exactly one year later.

# REFUELING

Captain L. was about to confirm an axiom of fighter flying I had learned twenty years earlier: "Night refueling is just like day refueling, except you can't see a ----ing thing!" This bit of wisdom had come from one of my legendary F-105 instructors in the 561st Tactical Fighter Squadron (TFS) in Kansas. It perfectly describes the perception if not the reality, as you prepare to perform this delicate aerial ballet in the dark for the first time.

Of course, all of the pilots and WSOs going to Libya had refueled at night many times before. And, thanks to the lengthening spring days, the first refuelings en route to Libya were being performed in twilight conditions. This allowed every crew to get used to the lighting and positioning cues on the McDonnell Douglas KC-10 Extender tankers. That was indeed fortunate. The crews were lucky to have this brief day-to-night transition because none of them had ever refueled from a KC-10 at night. KC-10s had been available in small numbers in Europe for months, but scheduling large formations for night tanker training had seemed to be too much of a giveaway to those watching us.

In many of the F-111 cockpits, completion of the first air refueling cycle signaled an opportunity to refuel their bodies as well. Following the flight surgeon's advice, many crewmen had dug into typical, greasy officers' club cheeseburgers as part of their pre-mission lunch. The idea was to eat meals that would have no major inflight effects on the crews' digestive systems. With minimal provisions for body functions—plastic "piddle packs" for urination are the only device available in a fighter—this was an important consideration. Surprisingly, the club fare was recommended for that purpose. Individuals met with varying degrees of success in this regard during the course of the thirteen-plus-hour mission. For inflight refreshment, pilots and their WSOs had chosen a wide variety of combinations to fight off both hunger and thirst. One pilot, a major, had stuffed a six-pack of 7UP under his seat, and promptly proceeded to partially crush it when he lowered his seat! Fortunately, the cans did not burst and were still useable—before the night was over, he would drink all six. A captain WSO was one of several who took along two full box lunches on the mission. He ate one during the pre-strike refuelings, and finished the other on the way back to England.

Food and drink, however, were not the only necessities for a mission of this length. Air Force crews are tested for their tolerance and reactions to both "stop" and "go" medications so that the individual can make a decision on when to use sleeping pills or amphetamines to prepare for and fly especially long sorties. Accordingly, all El Dorado Canyon F-111 crews were offered these drugs for their use. Some declined to take the pills from the flight surgeon—their experience with negative reactions dictated against their use. Others accepted, but with no certainty as to whether or not they would actually use them. As expected on this longest of all fighter combat missions, many eventually chose to take the "go" pills to help them stay alert. And several had taken sleeping pills to ensure some rest during the chaotic last twenty-four hours prior to takeoff.

Captain L. was not hungry, thirsty, or in need of any medication as he awaited his first turn on the tanker's boom; he was just nervous. The longer he waited, the more anxious he became: unlike the other pilots on the raid, Captain L. had never even seen a KC-10—day or night! To paraphrase my old instructor, refueling from one airplane is very much like refueling from any other, except for all the differences. Those include the unique formation cues for the tanker and the specific lighting arrangements for the tanker's fuselage, engine nacelles, and air refueling boom.

In an ideal training situation, the receiver pilot moves into position behind the tanker and then, knowing all of the lights that concern him, describes his personal menu of lighting requests using his radio. Captain L. knew he would not have that luxury. This mission was being flown "Comm Out"—without using the radios except for periodic brief status checks and real emergencies. Even if he had been able to talk to the tanker, his unfamiliarity with the KC-10's lighting would have prevented or delayed establishing a comfortable lighting arrangement. Like all the other crewmen, Captain L. would just have to suffer in silence—after all, this was combat.

As he jockeyed for a proper position behind and below the tanker, Captain L. concentrated on being smooth and predictable, ignoring the distractions presented by the array of dazzling lights above. Compared to the KC-135s he was used to, the KC-10 seemed too far away for a successful hookup. His legs pushed hard against both rudder pedals as he gritted his teeth, holding the pre-briefed position below the extra-long probe. Finally, he heard and felt the metallic clunk several feet behind him as the refueling boom automatically locked in position.

Five minutes later, he returned to the tanker's wing after successfully "learning by doing" how to refuel from a KC-10. His squadron commander had been right. When approached by Captain L., who had reluctantly admitted that he was a KC-10 virgin, the grizzled lieutenant colonel had sized up the young pilot, assessed the lack of time available to change crews, and assured him that he would be good at KC-10 refueling before the night was over.

Captain L.'s confidence grew through each of the six planned refuelings (four before the attack and two en route home), so that by the time the mission had ended, as predicted, he was an old pro at refueling from a KC-10 in the dark. Once beyond the Straits of Gibraltar, the refueling process required many more hookups for each aircraft. It became a continuous recycling process as each of the F-111s was kept nearly full of JP-8 jet fuel. This procedure ensured that each attacking jet would have as much fuel as possible when it reached its drop-off point. This would translate to increased fuel reserves later when the returning F-111s would be searching for their tankers in the dark. In practice, this continual refueling meant that every pilot was getting more training than he could possibly use that night—most counted between eight and twelve hookups to the tankers.

None of these multiple refuelings was any easier than the first—in fact, the later refuelings during the return flight to England were even more difficult and dangerous, as fatigued crews struggled to stay alert after almost ten hours of flying. The routine nature of air refueling operations masks the indisputable fact that they provide one of the biggest challenges faced by tactical aircrews. No single group of modern aviators ever faced a bigger refueling challenge than did the Tripoli raiders of 1986. And, as the pre-strike refuelings progressed, a problem arose that threatened to foul up the entire Air Force portion of Operation El Dorado Canyon.

## SEPTEMBER 1985

## THE ROYAL VISIT

If fate had not thrust the 48th Wing into combat in 1986, the biggest event of our tour of duty in England would almost certainly have been the royal visit. In the wake of the raid on Tripoli, Prince Charles's brief stop at our base seems little more than a footnote to the wing's big story. But it is an interesting footnote that helps explain peacetime life in a fighter wing, while introducing another character central to the story of the Air Force portion of El Dorado Canyon, Maj. Gen. Thomas G. McInerney.

The royal visit took place in September 1985, when His Royal Highness, the Prince of Wales came to RAF Lakenheath. Visits of royal family members to U.S. units based in the United Kingdom are relatively rare—this was the first for the 48th Wing in over fifteen years. Prince Charles had not visited a U.S. unit since 1982 when he toured our neighboring base at Mildenhall. As a result, we looked forward to His Royal Highness's arrival with great anticipation, knowing that all our people and their families would be thrilled and honored by the occasion.

Colonel Westbrook spent the entire month of August in the

United States, completing an executive management seminar at Columbia University in New York. A short vacation afterward delayed his return to Lakenheath until less than a week before Prince Charles's arrival. The result was that I had the responsibility for all preparations for the visit. And those preparations were at a level of detail that far surpassed what we might have done for any other VIP, except perhaps for our own president.

In preparation for the royal visit, our Royal Air Force station commander, Sqdn. Ldr. Mike Sharpe, provided the experience, and our base commander, Col. Dwight Kealoha, provided both manpower and close supervision. While their jobs were nominally similar in terms of both title and responsibility, Mike Sharpe's position was mostly symbolic. U.S. units stationed in Britain are considered to be tenants occupying what are really RAF bases. Therefore, RAF Lakenheath had to have an RAF station commander although he was the only member of his service stationed there. In any case, Mike's prior experience in hosting royal visits at other RAF stations proved to be essential as we wrestled with the necessary details. Working together, he and Colonel Kealoha came up with a second-by-second schedule for the prince which allowed him to see and be seen by as many Americans as possible. It also included a multiplane flyby of F-111Fs and an informal luncheon at the officers' club, after which Sam would present the prince with a gift as a token of our esteem. The overall goal was to ensure that the future king of England would leave our base after four hours with an excellent impression of our people and planes, not to mention the unit they constituted and the country they served.

The newly assigned Third Air Force commander, Maj. Gen. Thomas G. McInerney, took a strong personal interest in the royal visit. His previous experience in England had included a tour as air attache in the London embassy, as well as an assignment as the vice wing commander of the F-111-equipped 20th TFW at Upper Heyford. A graduate of West Point with a distinguished combat record and strong operational savvy, Major General McInerney understood the sensitivities associated with "colonists" hosting royalty. Not surprisingly, he wanted everything to be done with style and professionalism—all had to go well.

And it did! Despite the last-second hiccups likely in any complex plan, Prince Charles's visit was a total success. Though disappointed by Princess Diana's absence, the crowds at Lakenheath were large, friendly, and enthusiastic. Perhaps too enthusiastic—one of our young female schoolteachers lunged from the crowd to hug and kiss the surprised future monarch, but luckily did no permanent harm. Throughout the visit, His Royal Highness seemed to be enjoying himself, and his infectious good humor drew out the best in his audience. My wife Joyce was one of the few who seemed thunderstruck in his presence, but she recovered quickly after being presented to the prince. In the end, we said goodbye to Prince Charles and congratulated ourselves on having put on one of the best VIP tours ever witnessed at a U.S. base in England.

Knowing that I would have carried the lion's share of blame for any major foul-ups during the visit, I felt genuine relief and satisfaction when it all proved so successful. Major General McInerney and I had not served together before, so this small success was an excellent way for me to make a good first impression. He was the man who would largely determine a successor to Sam Westbrook in 1986, when the latter would be reassigned. And, as the sun set on September 12, 1985, he was, I hoped, as pleased as I was after the future king's visit to a major unit within his command.

Because of this initial triumph, I felt confident that Major General McInerney and I would not fall out on the cocktail circuit where much of our informal contact would occur. As expected, his daily interaction with his wings would be done through the commanders. As a vice commander, my personal contact with the general would be somewhat limited.

However, one of those early limited contacts may have been a portent of future problems. In speaking to several of his vice wing commanders about the state of U.S. officers' clubs in the U.K., Major General McInerney said that the club at RAF Greenham Common would serve as his command's standard for emulation. I was certain he was joking—the Greenham Lodge is a combination officers' club and VIP hotel housed in a historic 19th-century mansion. The building and its grounds are imposing, as is the interior renovation which the Air Force financed with an innovative combination of appropriated and non-appropriated funds in the early 1980s.

While there are better officers' clubs in terms of service and food, the Lodge at Greenham Common offers some of the most opulent VIP quarters available anywhere in the U.S. military. My first visit there prompted immediate thoughts of FWA, the well-known military acronym for "Fraud, Waste, and Abuse." At least, waste certainly seemed to apply. In any case, Major General McInerney's statement brought to mind improbable pictures of each of his vice wing commanders scrambling to find huge oaks for paneling and cut stone for exterior walls, while spending fantastic amounts of money to get it all done. I chuckled in response to what I was sure was a humorous comment by the general.

My laughter did not last long. The general replied that he was serious and that there was no reason we all could not provide facilities like the Greenham Manor to our people. They deserved to go first class, and we would have to do more to ensure that they did. The general's comments made me instantly aware that he was indeed serious. Chastened, I remained silent as the discussion continued, thinking all the time that only officers who had held flag rank entirely during the halcyon years of the Reagan presidency could easily form and hold such opinions. There is no doubt that President Reagan's military budgets did much to enhance our nation's security, as evidenced by 1991's Desert Storm, but more than a few dollars were used for purposes that did not directly provide combat capability. Significant sums of money were spent on the renovation of Air Force officers' clubs in England and elsewhere in Europe during the mid-eighties. The improvements that were made were certainly first class. Unfortunately, much of what was done was probably unnecessary.

Years later, questions would arise in Congress on the sources of the millions of dollars put into the Mildenhall club and other officers' clubs on the continent. A lengthy investigation into the specific problems at the Ramstein club in West Germany was quietly concluded in 1990 when letters of reprimand were issued to twelve unnamed officers and NCOs. As this story is written, that action is the only disciplinary measure that is likely to be taken in a case that involved the alleged illegal expenditure of millions of appropriated tax dollars. The Air Force now seems quite happy to let the matter rest.

Prince Charles's brief visit had served as a welcome diversion from the tedious business of preparing for war with the Warsaw Pact. But within hours of his departure, we were back at that task with a vengeance, flying nearly fifty training sorties each day to hone our skills. However, there was no great sense of urgency involved in their conduct; after all, the possibility of a large-scale war in Europe seemed very, very remote. And few of us envisioned any circumstance that would precipitate combat anywhere else in the world. The fall of 1985 seems an especially quaint time as viewed in retrospect from the summer of 1991.

# HIGH-SPEED REFUELING

Lieutenant Colonel C. was concerned. Flying aboard the lead KC-10 as part of Colonel Westbrook's staff, he had spent the first few hours of the mission helping to sort out various problems involving communications, air refueling, and spare aircraft. Three hours into the mission, as the aerial armada headed east having passed Gibraltar, he had begun to feel more relaxed. But something was worrying him: that last air refueling problem between a KC-135 and a KC-10 had taken quite a while to resolve. In addition, there had been some delay in the element of EF-111 jamming aircraft that took off from Upper Heyford.

His unease translated into a single crucial thought: was the mission still on schedule? But that thought did not prompt action until the pilot of the lead F-111F finally raised the alarm. During a routine radio and status check, Lieutenant Colonel F. ended his transmission with an emphatic "We're late!" (Some remember a oneword alarm: "Time!") Other F-111s chimed in with their concurrence, causing a trip to the KC-10's cockpit which confirmed Lieutenant Colonel C.'s worst fear—a major mistake had been made. The lead tanker and its F-111Fs slated to strike the Tripoli Airport were more than ten minutes behind schedule! If the error could not be corrected, the success of the entire mission was in jeopardy.

Timing was critical because what little surprise remained would vanish as the first bombs exploded. If the Navy strike force hit Benghazi on time and the Air Force was ten minutes late, Tripoli's defenses would be even better prepared. Also, the total time needed to attack the three Tripoli-area targets could be extended to over twenty minutes. Finally, the support forces, including Air Force EF-111 jamming aircraft, Navy EA-6B jammers, and Navy F/A-18 defense suppressors, would be partially wasted. They would expose themselves on schedule in support of forces that were, in some cases, still many miles from their targets. By the time the bombers arrived, the support forces would be low on fuel, out of ammunition, or both. Any of these events would increase the probability that Lakenheath F-111Fs might be hit or even shot down.

A 48th Wing captain had been in the cockpit of the lead KC-10, but had not taken decisive action to keep the attack force on schedule. The commanders onboard, Maj. Gen. David C. Forgan, the USAFE deputy commander for operations, and Colonel Westbrook, had been aware early in the flight that the actual winds were not as forecast, and that the task force was falling behind schedule. No immediate response was thought to be necessary; if the winds changed to approximate the forecast, only a brief acceleration would be required to correct the problem. Besides, if they had speeded up too early it could have caused the armada to get ahead of schedule—in that event, there was no good way to slow the force. That rationale proved correct for a while, but the task force gradually fell further behind schedule while other matters held the attention of the commanders and their staff.

As Lieutenant Colonel C. acknowledges today, the blame for the error cannot be easily placed. He was partially correct in suspecting the KC-135-to-KC-10 refueling problem; it had certainly caused some delay. But there had been other problems as well: during departure due to procedures necessitated by the runway change at Mildenhall; and later when EF-111s from Upper Heyford were delayed in joining the formation. In addition, as mentioned above, the winds encountered that night were not as favorable as had been predicted. That may confirm the simplest theory as to why the task force was late: tankers do their planning using true airspeed while fighters do theirs using ground speed. The two are only equal when there is no wind. However, all of these factors combined were still not enough to explain why the problem had not been recognized and corrected earlier. The fact of the matter appears to be that this important detail—the necessity of reaching the fighter drop-off points at a specific time—was just forgotten in the last-minute surge of activity that the mission generated. As one of the KC-10 tanker pilots recalls, he was not told of a requirement to make a specific drop-off point at a specified time until the El Dorado Canyon force had reached the vicinity of the Straits of Gibraltar.

For whatever reason, no one from the 48th had adequately stressed to the KC-10 tanker crews that the drop-off points *had to* be reached on schedule. It was briefed to them as a priority, but as only one of many competing priorities that night. In the face of stronger-than-expected headwinds and the previously mentioned refueling and rendezvous problems, the lead KC-10 had gradually fallen further and further behind schedule. While almost everyone was aware that a problem was developing, no decisive action had been taken until it was almost too late. Now, with less than two hours' flight time remaining to the drop-off point in the central Mediterranean, something had to be done quickly to correct the problem. It was time for some high-speed air refueling.

Air refueling is typically conducted at comfortable airspeeds in the mid-range of an aircraft's operating envelope. According to the F-111F's book, the "Dash One" bible that every flight crew tries to memorize, those speeds are in the ballpark of 300 to 325 knots indicated airspeed. At higher speeds, the controls get more sensitive—"goosey" is the fighter pilot's term—and refueling becomes more difficult. In addition, the combat-loaded Aardvark also requires almost constant use of afterburner on at least one engine during the high-speed hookups. The increased thrust is necessary just to keep from falling off the tanker's boom as the receiving jet's weight increases. It also aggravates the problem of goosey controls since the preferred technique—setting the throttle on the engine in afterburn and using the other throttle to control speed—causes the jet to yaw. An additional effect of all this extra afterburner is that the tanker's planned fuel reserves are further depleted. The reduced tanker fuel states would cause difficulties hours later in the mission.

But on April 14, 1986, despite these predictable problems, it was time to throw away the book: those ten minutes had to be made up! At Lieutenant Colonel C.'s immediate urging, the armada accelerated, while simultaneously turning to cut off the minor dogleg that remained in their planned course. Their new course would come uncomfortably close to violating the territorial airspace of some noninvolved countries, but it was essential to the catch-up plan now being hastily formulated. The new course had one other disadvantage: it put several planned radar offset points out of range of the F-111Fs' radars. Following the original flight plan would have allowed the crews to keep their inertial navigation systems accurately updated. The catch-up course meant that the 48th's F-111 crews would grow increasingly uncertain of their exact positions—a very uncomfortable feeling when trying to find pinpoint targets at the end of a 2,500-mile flight. It seems probable that this uncertainty later contributed to a series of small mistakes that caused the unintended, tragic collateral damage on the raid.

As the delicate refueling maneuvers continued at airspeeds approaching 400 knots, some F-111 crews silently cursed the tanker crews whom they mistakenly blamed for the entire problem. But they also breathed a sigh of relief as it became clear that they would make, though just barely, their planned drop-off times. However, because of the error, they would be operating at airspeeds much higher than normal for up to two hours. Flying night formation and refueling at these speeds was anything but fun. As the mission passed its fourth hour, the force bound for Tripoli raced across the Mediterranean, gradually making up the lost ten minutes. This was just one more part of the difficult set of circumstances that would make Operation El Dorado Canyon such a memorable mission for those who flew it—and survived.

**DECEMBER 1985–JANUARY 1986**

**INITIAL WARNING ORDERS:**

**A NEW KIND OF CONTINGENCY**

The end-of-year holiday season had been in full swing for weeks, but the mood was not entirely festive for any American living in Europe as 1985 drew to a close. At Lakenheath, we were still celebrating the announcement that Colonel Westbrook would soon become a brigadier general—Sam was on his way to the four stars we were certain he deserved. However, the simultaneous terrorist attacks on the Rome and Vienna airports on December 27 had shocked us all back to immediate realities. Twenty Americans had been killed, and there were scores of other Americans among the wounded. U.S. military units throughout Europe stood at heightened states of alert. However, the primary focus of these alerts was to prevent further attacks against U.S. military personnel and their families. Speculation concerning a U.S. military response to the slaughters in Rome and Vienna was widespread, but two days passed without substantive action taking place. Finally, on December 30, 1985, top secret initial warning orders were issued from Washington. The 48th Wing at Lakenheath was one of the few Air Force units to receive those orders, sent under the initial operational code name "Prime Pump."

Arriving at Lakenheath in the first hours of the New Year, the substance of the initial orders was for our wing to begin preparations to strike any of a short list of targets in Libya within a relatively short time frame. The first messages asked more questions than they answered, inquiring about a variety of issues associated with a retaliatory raid. When would we be ready to conduct such a mission? What ordnance would we suggest against a specific target? How many tankers would we require in support of a chosen route of flight? The questions went on and on, as did our answers. New Year's Day was spent formulating our first response to these questions, and trying to gauge the probabilities that the initial plans would be executed immediately. The latter was a "crystal ball" exercise in which we had limited success: no one could know for certain whether or not we would be attacking in hours, days, weeks, or even months. Based on our cumulative experience, it seemed likely that we would not be attacking at all.

Contingencies are a fact of life for any military organization. Planning for possible responses to a particular set of circumstances is something that almost all military units are asked to do on a regular, recurring basis. Anyone who has served in a combat unit for any length of time has been through the drill again and again. While each contingency is guaranteed to differ from its predecessors in almost every way, there is one factor that they all share: the extremely high probability that a given contingency plan will not be put into action. We were all well aware of the odds that our first plans for "Prime Pump" would go the way of so many before them, ending up somewhere in a classified file cabinet awaiting disposal. We wrestled with this fact while appraising the saber rattling emanating from Washington—as 1986 began, the outrage over Rome and Vienna was still palpable. It appeared for a time that we would, indeed, be bombing Libya within days.

However, as each day passed without an order to attack, that likelihood rapidly diminished. The countries sponsoring the airport terrorists had not been positively identified. Could responsibility be determined within the half-life of our national indignation over the attacks? The 48th Wing's primary concern, of course, was to build a viable strike plan and to stand prepared to execute it. Nevertheless, we could not help but evaluate the odds that those orders would be issued. And that calculation led to a decision by Colonel Westbrook that would very much affect both of our roles in relation to the eventual raid on Libya.

Several months earlier, Sam had scheduled a skiing trip to Austria for early January. With his family gathered for the holidays, reservations and deposits made, and the joys of Scheffau's slopes beckoning, Sam consulted with Maj. Gen. McInerney as to whether he could risk being absent from Lakenheath for two weeks. The general shared Sam's view that while nothing was certain, it was unlikely that the raid would be executed so quickly that Colonel Westbrook could not return from Austria in time to take command of his wing. Preliminary travel arrangements would be made with USAFE headquarters to ensure that this was feasible. In the meantime, I would be left in command of the 48th and the continuing contingency planning efforts. Whether or not it was justified, I took their mutual decision as a vote of confidence in my ability to handle the situation. This and other required absences by Colonel Westbrook would eventually put me in acting command of the wing for five of the fifteen weeks that led up to the mission. They would prove to be eventful, interesting weeks!

On January 2, as Sam and I "shook the stick" (Air Force slang for transferring control, indicative of the cockpit practice), we had no idea that the bombs would not drop on Libya until over three months had passed. We also were unaware that the "action" had already started on the media front where "bombs" were being dropped on what was supposed to be a top secret plan.

We had responded to receipt of our preparatory orders with extreme attention to security. Only a few people within the wing—less than two dozen—were brought into the planning process. In order to tap wing resources in other areas, many others were told only the scantest details relating directly to their areas of expertise. For example, a few officers and senior NCOs in the munitions maintenance squadron were ordered to have certain types and numbers of weapons available for immediate loading. They were told little else. All in all, the 48th Wing responded to the security aspects of the possible impending raid with the attitude you would expect of a frontline unit. After all, it would be our men and our planes that would be at risk if the mission was flown. Throughout the period that led up to the raid, we did our best to keep every aspect of it very close-hold. It was a potential top secret mission; we treated it as such. We also naively expected that others within our government would do the same. We were about to discover the realities of the war against terrorism.

The crews of the 48th who flew the raid were certainly not the first U.S. airmen to attack alerted targets. Veterans of the 100th Bomb Group (Heavy) often recall that during World War II, "Axis Sally" regularly welcomed them to their particular target on the day of a mission—as they crossed the English Channel eastbound![1] It undoubtedly went something like this: "Best wishes today to the men of the 100th Group in their B-17s. Our Luftwaffe gunners and fighter aircraft look forward to greeting you over Münster this morning. You would be wise to abort now and return to your base at Thorpe Abbotts!" While these announcements were generally greeted with derision, they were often uncomfortably accurate in specifying the day's actual target. Maybe that is why the 100th Group and so many of its sister units took terrible losses on so many missions over the Third Reich.

But even the veterans of World War II have been surprised to find out just how much notice Colonel Qaddafi received. As we would discover much later, tongues were already wagging in Washington before New Year's Day, 1986.

On December 31, 1985, the NBC nightly news telecast included a report from Jim Miklaszewski concerning ongoing interest in Libya at the Pentagon. His comments mentioned "Pentagon sources" who indicated that planning had been underway for a year for actions that ". . . include air strikes against terrorist camps in Libya." On January 1, the *Baltimore Sun* repeated and reinforced the NBC version in a front page article entitled "Reagan Is Sent List of Military Options by Joint Chiefs." Had we known of either of these reports in England, we probably would not have been too concerned. After all, they were not very specific, and they made no mention of how such attacks might be made. Our planning in what we thought was total secrecy continued.

By January 2, Qaddafi had read the papers and the tea leaves, and proceeded to make an inflammatory statement that Libya would attack "Americans in their own streets" if the U.S. retaliated against Libya for the airport attacks in December. He undoubtedly hoped to prevent such an attack by intimidation. While he failed to intimidate, he did succeed in gaining information because of his intemperance.

On January 3, the *Washington Post* reported on its front page that President Reagan had fired back, denouncing "fellows who think it's all right to shoot eleven-year-old girls." The remainder of the article included some details, provided by unnamed "informed sources," of just how such a raid could be executed. Libyans throughout the world had to turn all the way to page two to discover that the carrier USS *Coral Sea* was in the Mediterranean, that U.S.-based B-52s were an option, and that "F-111 bombers at British bases at Lakenheath and Upper Heyford" could be used. That night, the CBS evening news telecast repeated the report that Air Force jets based in Great Britain were being considered in the planning, but with an added twist. David Martin indicated that his Pentagon sources said that these jets were ". . . one of the leading options for attacking Libya." Those sources, Martin said, went on to explain that "[the F-111s] are equipped for low-level nighttime runs with laser guided bombs" and that the Libyan Air Force had "only a rudimentary night flying capability."

It had taken less than four days for Lakenheath and our F-111s to be specifically identified as a possible option for a strike against Libyan support of terrorism. In fact, use of F-111s was not just any option; it was one of the leading options! And apparently to prove their credibility, the government/Pentagon sources had gone so far as to reveal our likely tactics and time of attack! Meanwhile in Suffolk, we reviewed our short target list and our detailed plans in blissful ignorance and great secrecy. The New Year was about to enter its fourth day.

On January 4, the words of those accommodating sources at the Pentagon finally reached us in East Anglia. That night, I was startled to see the BBC broadcast a tape of David Martin's CBS report from the previous evening, accompanied by videotape of F-111s taking off and landing. The British commentator also specifically mentioned both Lakenheath and Upper Heyford. I was more than shocked; I was appalled. Crews from the 48th Wing were already prepared to strike Libya within hours of an order from their commander in chief. Somehow, the fact that they might get that order had already become public knowledge. The situation raised a single overriding question: how many of our men might die because of this breach of security?

My indignation would be short-lived, however. The realities of a peacetime pseudowar against shadowy terrorists would be brought home to me in no uncertain terms and beginning immediately. January 5 dawned with reports from our wing security police that television crews from the BBC, British independent television, and all of the major U.S. networks were deployed along the A-1065 roadway that borders RAF Lakenheath's main base and the runway. Cameras were rolling continuously as the media, anticipating an imminent U.S. raid from Britain against Libya, jockeyed for the best pictures of the takeoff. Phones were also busy throughout the day as we sought and received guidance from above on how to handle the situation. As you would expect in any liberal democracy, the options were limited. Short of an invocation of the British Official Secrets Act (not an option for a U.S. wing commander), nothing could be done to inhibit the press or the broadcast media. After much consultation, we were essentially told to learn to live with the situation.

That status quo lasted for less than forty-eight hours, however. By January 7, the U.S. media representatives and their camera crews had sought, and gained, permission to enter our base. They had also asked to conduct interviews, but our protests had spared us at least that requirement. That day, Maj. John "Terry" Tyrrell, our chief of public affairs, and his staff accompanied a group of media people on a brief chaperoned tour of our facilities. Pictures were taken, questions were asked, succinct answers were given, but no interview took place with anyone in a position to know anything about the top secret planning and preparation for the raid. As we escorted our media friends out RAF Lakenheath's gate that afternoon, we did not know that their first feeding frenzy regarding the mission was about to end. The reason for this change in attitude was that the odds against an immediate strike on Libya were rapidly going up.

By January 8, news reports were out that the president had decided to limit his response against suspected Libyan involvement in terrorism to diplomatic and economic measures—the military option had been rejected. The reasons for this decision, as reported by Bernard Gwertzman in the *New York Times*, were the "unacceptable risks" posed by "the fate of more than 1,000 Americans in Libya, an outbreak of explosive anti-Americanism in Arab countries, and the possibility that American planes could be downed over Libya."

The first of the three concerns was certainly valid and, in my estimation, was the primary reason why no U.S. attack was ordered against Libya in January 1986. Later, U.S. citizens would be directed to leave Libya or risk suffering the consequences. But in January they were there in large numbers, and they could easily have become just so many hostages if we had attacked.

The last reason given for not bombing, the possible loss of U.S. aircraft, was the least convincing in our view. Despite the public announcements of a likely attack's timing and tactics, the small raid that we had ready for execution in January would have probably succeeded without loss. The crews who were prepared to fly shared this opinion. They were convinced that the high-speed, low-altitude attacks they were practicing would make them almost invulnerable. They were sure that the Libyans did not know their exact targets, nor the precise timing and direction of the planned bombing runs—they would have tactical surprise, even though strategic surprise had been lost forever due to those ubiquitous Pentagon sources. They were also certain that the Libyan defenses were not fully prepared nor properly deployed to meet such an attack—at least not yet. In our crews' overstated view, if the raid had been ordered in January, they would have been refueling on their way home to Lakenheath before a significant Libyan defensive reaction would have taken place.

The few 48th TFW pilots and WSOs then involved believed all of this partially because Col. Tom Yax, the deputy commander for operations, and I tried to convince them of it. The BBC reports and the highly visible media attention had understandably shaken them. Knowledge that the raid was to an extent preannounced had given them reason to be concerned. Colonel Yax and I assured them that they still had tactical surprise with which they could safely do the job. If nothing else, these short pep talks served to increase the motivation for security within the wing; it was up to us to protect our men by protecting the list of targets, attack options, and likely Times Over Target (TOTs). Hopefully, the Pentagon gang would be less forthcoming with these details than they had been with the basic information on Aardvark tactics and capabilities!

By the second week in January, the wing was beginning a gradual return to normalcy. While we were still on alert for a possible attack, tension had begun to decrease as the likelihood of the mission being ordered seemed to diminish. We were not fully aware of the ongoing debates in the White House and at the Pentagon, but we could feel the changes occurring as each additional day passed and the stark images of the Rome and Vienna terrorist attacks faded from memory. As we prepared for Sam Westbrook's return from Austria, it would have been easy to breathe a sigh of relief were it not for one incident that had occurred in the middle of the media circus that went on between January 5 and 7.

The media's continual presence and smothering attention during that first week in January had already convinced us that the

48th was in what is commonly called a "whole new ball game." This was not going to be anything like our normal peacetime operation, nor would it resemble any other contingency we had experienced. Highly classified plans and operations are not supposed to attract instant worldwide publicity. With Sam Westbrook skiing in Austria and not due back for ten more days, we had wrestled with the limited options available to handle the media situation. We were now about to find out, in a very different way, just how extraordinary this contingency was. What I will call the "twenty-hour option" was revealed.

The twenty-hour option was a plan to strike a specific target on a round-trip mission from Lakenheath that would involve approximately twenty hours' flying time for the tasked F-111s. The details of the proposed mission were contained in a message that reached us like any other message in the flood of Special Category (SPECAT) communications that had begun in late December. The fact that the specified source of the message was a USAFE staff agency at our headquarters in West Germany meant little to us—a combat unit on alert for possible execution of a national contingency assumes that any inquiry comes from sources at or near "National Command Authorities," a collective term for the president and the secretary of defense. As a result, we took on the task of responding to this option with all the seriousness of combat—depending on our reply, we could be striking the new targets within seventy-two hours.

Since the message allowed the wing less than twenty-four hours to reply and was not addressed to our intermediate headquarters at Third Air Force, we produced a reply entirely within the wing and without reference to the Third Air Force staff at Mildenhall (only five miles away). At this point, only Major General McInerney and a few members of his staff were cleared to receive information on Prime Pump. From an operational command standpoint, there was no direction to include a numbered Air Force in the closely held planning process for a contingency. In fact, the precedents that we knew of specifically excluded intermediate headquarters in the interest of both security and simplicity. Time proved that this guidance was still valid: Third Air Force was not addressed in any SPECAT message until late March, and then only at the secret level. The first SPECAT top secret message regarding the operation was not addressed to Mildenhall until after the raid. None of this changed the fact that Third Air Force was still in business just a stone's throw to the west of Lakenheath. Based on the complexity of our reply and the urgency in drafting it, the general would not be briefed until after we had responded.

Our reply was complex because the twenty-hour option was unlike any we had previously contemplated. The January 5, 1986, message from Ramstein posed this question: given a short list of distant targets (locations are still classified; they are unimportant to this story) and assuming denial of overflight rights by our allies, how would the 48th TFW attack on a round-trip mission exceeding twenty hours' duration? As Colonel Yax and I digested the query, we came to several shared conclusions.

First, the details of the mission, including tanker support, detailed attack plans, etc., would take several hours to complete and translate into a message. With our reply due early the next morning, we assigned a group of wing planners to work through the night to perform that task. Second, the targets and their known defenses dictated that a small, uncomplicated night raid remained the best option, despite the strategic warning being provided by the western media. Finally—and fatefully—we decided that the potential complications of a mission of this length had to be fully acknowledged in our reply.

We had considered the possible stresses on our crews and aircraft posed by a twelve- to fourteen-hour flight, but none of us had thought about the problems of a much longer mission. What would be the impact on weapons delivery systems, electronic warfare pods, basic flight instruments, and engines? Obvious questions, like what quantity of oil would remain in each engine, had to be answered. As to the crews, none of us could fully appreciate just what they would go through. As a veteran of an 8.9-hour combat mission in the F-105, I had some idea of the stresses involved. How would our guys perform on a night mission more than twice that length? No one knew and no one wanted to guess. We ultimately agreed that a paragraph of real-world caveats would have to be included in order to give National Command Authorities the total picture. We settled on 6:30 the next morning as a good time to review the reply message before sending it at 8 A.M.

The reply that Tom presented for my signature on January 6 contained everything that I had requested. A detailed, small-scale attack was outlined, along with a conservative estimate of the substantial air refueling tanker requirements. Having told in detail how we would do it if so ordered, the message concluded with a paragraph listing the likely problems that could interfere with that success. Among others, crew exhaustion, major equipment failures, and engine malfunctions were all mentioned. A final sentence included a commander's assessment, mine, that based on the combination of factors cited, a fighter mission of this length might well be considered to be "infeasible."

In retrospect, that word was obviously a poor choice. After all, the bulk of our message stated the wing's plan for performing the twenty-hour mission—how could we simultaneously conclude that it could not be done? Of course, what we had meant was that this option should not be selected—its probability of success was too low and the risks were too high. But I should have considered the semantics involved. That became clear later when we briefed Major General McInerney on the USAFE message and our reply.

We gathered in the wing command post at about 7 P.M. on January 6, to brief the general on the situation. Things went well until he began reading the final paragraph of our message. While he read in silence, his demeanor gradually betrayed his increasing agitation. When he finished his review, he asked that we discuss the matter further in the privacy of our battle cab. Privacy is a relative term though: Colonel Yax and two of our lieutenant colonels joined us in that room.

The elevated glassed-in battle cab, where the wing's leaders keep their fingers on the pulse of the unit, is almost soundproof with the doors secured. Nevertheless, it was probably not insulated well enough to contain the lively discussion that ensued as the general critiqued our reply to USAFE. Who had signed out this inaccurate message? he asked. How could we have replied with such a negative, unenthusiastic assessment of our wing's capabilities? Why had we speculated on so many possible malfunctions when there was always a chance that everything would go well? And, finally, who had decided to include the word "infeasible?" With the way the last question was asked, there was little doubt that the general did not intend to congratulate the author.

I acknowledged my responsibility for signing out the message and for including the offending word. I also attempted to defend the rest of the message as based on the facts as I saw them. We were not being negative: we were being realistic in portraying the problems that were probable, not just possible, on a twenty-hour mission. Yes, there was a chance that everything would go well, but my experience told me that that was very unlikely. Those of us who have had to abandon burning multimillion-dollar jets in flight appreciate the limits of technology. During this very animated discussion, Tom Yax chimed in on my behalf, defending the message over which his staff had labored all night. Meanwhile, the two lieutenant colonels nervously tried to blend in with the room's furniture. Their discomfort and reticence was understandable—being present during the dressing-down of a senior officer was inappropriate, as would have been any comment on their part.

Our defense of the wing's position did not satisfy Major General McInerney. Where had all the real fighter pilots gone, he asked; the ones with the "Can Do," "Gung Ho" attitudes? Maybe they were all down the road at Upper Heyford in the 20th Wing, he suggested. His previous units in the Pacific, like the 3d Wing at Clark or the 8th at Kunsan, would have eagerly performed this mission without a second thought. As a matter of fact, if the 48th couldn't handle this mission, he was certain some other, less cautious outfit could. If necessary, he would lead the mission himself. The implication was that, at the very least, he would get someone to provide positive leadership to the 48th TFW. If the current bunch could not do it, he would find someone from outside the wing who could.

Major General McInerney's comments about the wing in comparison to other fighter units had a predictable effect: he was no longer the only angry man in the command post. His remarks seemed insulting both to me personally and to the 48th TFW. But I also recognized that his last statements posed a direct, unmistakable threat. When and if Sam Westbrook left the wing in May, as scheduled, I fully intended to be his successor. Suddenly that prospect was severely threatened by a single word within a single message. Something had to be done to alleviate the situation.

I pointed out that the bulk of our message had outlined a plan for executing the twenty-hour option, and that we were willing and able to do just that if ordered. I had included a paragraph on potential problems because, as the commander of the unit that might have to perform the mission, I believed it was my responsibility to do so. That dual responsibility was both to those who might order the mission and to those who might fly it. Yes, *infeasible* was a strong, perhaps wrong, word; but the line had to be drawn somewhere as to what should be considered a feasible mission duration for fighter aircraft. I had drawn the line between thirteen and twenty hours; the general might not draw it until somewhere between twenty and twenty-five hours. As professional military officers, we disagreed on where to draw the line, but the point was that it must be drawn.

The stance we had taken in our message would also apply some pressure to the chain of command to provide overflight rights or forward basing. Either of these actions would do much to ensure the mission's success. In a manner that I hoped was both calm and convincing, I gave our rationale for including a paragraph that, admittedly, was not brimming with optimism. The general replied with a surprising change in the direction in our discussion.

Messages like the one we had sent, he suggested, could prevent the Air Force from ever achieving its force goal of forty fighter wings—instead, the Navy might end up with more carriers. Again, the implication of his statement was instantly clear. The Navy had been the exclusive prosecutor of national policy in the Mediterranean for many months. For the first time, options were being considered which would give the Air Force a piece of the action against our terrorist enemies. In the wake of our negative message, there was the possibility that those options would be abandoned, eliminating the use of land-based tactical air power from the equation. Without such visible demonstrations of our usefulness and effectiveness, the Congress could very well reduce funding for Air Force fighter aircraft while adding money for more carrier battle groups.

Only the general's manner made me realize that he was, indeed, serious. I was momentarily stumped as to what to do in the face of my supposed sabotage of the future of the United States Air Force. His thoughts, I realized, were probably appropriate for a potential four-star general versed in Air Force ideology and alert to any interservice implication. I was just the acting commander of a single fighter wing which was now on alert for imminent combat. But even granting that Major General McInerney was right about the budgetary implications, I felt that it did not change the need for a frank overall assessment of our chances to reach National Command Authorities.

The lengthy, sometimes heated discussion ended at that point, with the general emphasizing the need for his review of all future outgoing messages on this contingency, if at all possible before they left the wing. His insistence on direct involvement did not track with the fact that he was not being included as an addressee on Prime Pump messages. Nevertheless, it was obvious that Third Air Force would be continuously involved from this point on. My hope was that McInerney's close observation of our future actions would repair the damage that had been done that day. Later events would prove how futile that hope was.

There are two ironic footnotes to this story. The first is that the twenty-hour option did not originate in the White House or the National Security Council. "National Command Authorities," in this instance, turned out to be a major on the USAFE contingency planning staff. This officer, a competent professional and a very good friend, had initiated the query in anticipation of an option he considered likely, but which was discarded almost immediately by whomever had proposed it. Our reply message never reached a level where the 48th's "defeatist attitude" could have caused the major repercussions that concerned the general. Then again, perhaps it did—less than two years after the raid, the Air Force gave up its goal of forty fighter wings while the Navy gained two carriers! Never underestimate the impact of a single written word.

The second irony is that after the raid, when hindsight clearly validated our concerns about the length of the mission, Third Air Force took a stance nearly identical to the one the 48th Wing had taken on January 5. By the end of April, Major General

McInerney was firmly established as the operational commander of any subsequent contingency action that might involve units based in the United Kingdom. Asked in April to evaluate an option that required a seventeen-hour round trip, his command replied with a message that was practically a carbon copy of the one we had sent in January.

I take no pleasure in the fact that all of the problems anticipated on a twenty-hour mission, listed in detail in our message of January 6, turned out to have major impacts on the actual, fourteen-hour mission flown three months later. Crews suffered from fatigue and stress, and, as a result, made mistakes; weapons delivery sensors malfunctioned, causing bombs which had been carried 2,500 miles not to be dropped; aircraft systems failed, contributing to other aborted bomb runs and nearly causing the loss of an additional F-111F.

It did not take great prescience to predict these difficulties: the probabilities derived from long experience with the Aardvark practically guaranteed these results on the longest fighter mission in history. Nevertheless, their inclusion in our message had prompted one serious butt-chewing for this old colonel. The commander in chief of USAFE, Gen. Charles L. Donnelly, had long ago adopted as his theme a line from an old Johnny Mercer's tune that says you have to "Accentuate the positive." I had just received a practical, real-world lesson as to what that meant to one of his protégés. Later on I would come to understand his interpretation of the song's next line, "Eliminate the negative."

# FIVE

# FINAL CHECKS

The pressure of events was having a clarifying effect on Captain N.'s mind. Earlier in the mission, during departure and the multiple refuelings, he had found himself distracted by a tumble of thoughts unrelated to the raid. Now, however, he was completely absorbed in the tasks involved in staying alive until reaching the target.

After leaving the KC-10 tanker, "Puffy-11" had turned to a southerly heading and rapidly descended to an altitude of less than 500 feet above the water. Speeding across Qaddafi's "Line of Death" in the Gulf of Sidra, he and his pilot concentrated on the automatic terrain-following system which was controlling their altitude using inputs primarily from the radar altimeter. This mode of operation would continue until they approached land, when the system would revert to its primary method of operation, comparing forward-looking radar returns with projected flight path information based on heading, winds, and airspeed. In that mode and assuming all was well, it would continuously monitor altitude, ordering climbs or dives as necessary to ensure that the selected terrain clearance was not violated—if the crew selected 500 feet, that was as low as the system would allow them to go.

The pilot's hand hung loosely just behind the stick, prepared to apply immediate back pressure to start a climb for survival if any system malfunction was discovered. Captain N. helped in this essential monitoring, while also attending to navigation. Selected Offset Aim Points (OAPs), both natural terrain features and man-made objects, appeared on his radar scope, allowing him to update the inertial navigation system. Even the best inertial navigators accumulate small errors over time; the F-111F's system drifted about a quarter of a mile an hour. Without update, "Puffy-11" could have been well off course after over five hours of flight. These periodic updates kept the errors small enough so that the target would appear where and when it was expected on the attack radar screen. Without them, the crew was unlikely to find the target at all. At least one of the Tripoli raiders was forced to abort its attack for that exact reason. And, unfortunately, one other attacker probably should have aborted but did not.

"Puffy-11" and the other five F-111Fs in line behind it each received a "tickle," a momentary indication that radar energy was reaching the aircraft, on its warning equipment as the Libyan SA-5 radar at Sirte searched the night skies. Unperturbed—they were well out of range of any missiles from the site—the crews descended to a slightly lower altitude and the signal disappeared. They continued toward the Libyan coast. One of the six aircraft aborted, turning northbound to rejoin its tanker. That plane's terrain-following radar system had failed, preventing it from completing the overland portion of the approach to its target, the Tripoli Airport. It was one of several varied system failures that would plague the Lakenheath F-111Fs that night. They were beginning to reveal themselves as the crews completed their final checks en route to their targets.

The systems that required checking included the inertial navigation system, the attack radar, the terrain-following system, the defensive electronic warfare system, the Pave Tack FLIR and laser designator, and, most importantly, the weapons release panel switches. These components and others were evaluated during a comprehensive "fence check," the last look at needed high-tech marvels before the stress of combat prevents any further analysis of what is or is not working. Each crew did a fence check, hoping that no glitches would appear. If a problem in their aircraft's systems was revealed, this was the time to know about it. The crew could then make a decision either to abort or to continue. The latter was unlikely: too many potential problems would violate the stringent ROE. The hope in every cockpit was that no last-second, hair-on-fire, major malfunction would occur. A few crews had no such luck.

For most of the crews with "good jets"—those with fully functioning systems—the challenge of a successful Pave Tack Toss maneuver would be the last hurdle encountered in trying to put their bombs on their assigned targets. For the delivery of most weapons, the toss maneuver was the preferred method for the Pave Tack–equipped F-111F, and it would be used against two of the three targets at Tripoli. As the attack force bore down on Tripoli, pilots and WSOs reviewed the intricacies of this maneuver, one that they all had practiced hundreds of times both in the actual aircraft and in the ground computerized simulator.

In the toss, the aircraft approaches its target at low altitude and high speed. Based on the ballistics of the weapons carried, a fairly abrupt pull-up begins at a preplanned distance from the target. The nose continues up to a specific pitch attitude, or until the bombs are automatically released, typically fifteen-to-thirty degrees up. Now nose-high climbing toward the target, the pilot initiates a hard turn away after weapons release. He pulls the nose back down so that he can rapidly return to the sanctuary of low altitude—missiles and bullets cannot hit a jet hidden in a valley. But this is not done too quickly—the ground is rushing up, trying to kill him, so the return to automatic terrain following in the dark must be done gingerly. The WSO's help is crucial to this task, but is only available after he has guided the bomb precisely to its target.

Navigation to the target and its radar identification are also his responsibilities. Once the nose has started up, the WSO switches from radar to FLIR, trying to identify the target so that he can place laser energy directly on it. Having acquired the target and activated the laser, he keeps his head firmly in his scopes during the plane's maneuvers, struggling to keep the laser spot exactly on the aim point until the bomb impact. At that point, with survival as as a strong motivating factor, he joins the pilot in executing both the tricky return to automatic terrain following and the speedy departure from the target area. To use the fighter pilot's vernacular, they do their very best to "Get out of Dodge," unharmed by the defenses or the unseen ground close below. At combat speeds, the Pave Tack Toss, from pull-up to bomb impact, takes place in less than forty-five seconds. During that short interval, there are a thousand ways to screw it up.

A few of those errors can be fatal, but most of them will just make the bombs miss their target. The pilot may pull too hard and the laser beam will be obscured by the plane's tail. Or the WSO may aim the laser at the wrong point or even forget to turn it on. Any of these errors, and too many more to mention, will result in a miss rather than a hit. Since most missions into the teeth of sophisticated defenses utilize a single attack (a tactic known as "one pass; haul ass"), one small error can totally ruin the entire mission. System failures and malfunctions are an entirely different matter—they are beyond the crew's control. But if the attack fails because of their error, the crew will live with the knowledge that they exposed their fragile bodies and expensive aircraft to hostile fire for no good reason. No one going to Azziziyah Barracks or the Sidi Balal terrorist training camp that night wanted to have that happen after having carried their bombs over 2,500 miles for delivery to Qaddafi's Libya.

Captain N. aimed his laser designator at a tower along his route of flight to check that the laser was firing and that it was aligned with the reticle he used to point it. In peacetime, laser "firings" are often simulated; there are too many concerns about possible dangers to people, animals, and property despite the low level of energy involved. As a result, this system is not used, checked, and calibrated as often as other routinely utilized components, such as the attack radar. Captain N. was pleased that his laser system was functioning normally with almost perfect alignment of the beam with his aiming reticle. While the bombs he carried, twelve Mark-82 "Airs," were not laser guided, he would use the laser for final ranging to the target. This would provide the most accurate delivery possible from the low-altitude, level attack profile they had planned. Safe delivery of these 500-pound bombs from low altitude was possible because they were "retarded" by air-inflated, parachute-like devices which gave them their nickname, "Airs," and which slowed them after release from the jet, allowing the speeding aircraft to get away from the blast and fragments of the exploding bomb.

As another F-111F sped toward its target at Azziziyah Barracks, the first in a series of small errors was made which would eventually result in the unintended deaths of Libyan civilians. The WSO had been unable to get an update to his inertial navigation system due to the shortcut his tanker had taken to ensure that the force was on time. After leaving the tanker, he had correctly updated his plane's position in relation to a small island—the last such checkpoint before the Libyan coast. What no one including this capable WSO knew then was that the "known" location of the island he had used for his update was apparently incorrect by several hundred feet. The coordinates for that inconspicuous piece of land were not "mensurated": placed precisely using exact cartographic and satellite measuring techniques.

That oversight contributed to several unsuccessful bomb runs in the El Dorado Canyon attack force, but by itself it may or may not have been enough to cause this particular crew to miss their target. However, they were now approaching landfall where the final update of the navigation system, essential to target acquisition, would occur. At that point, a second small mistake occurred when the radar was kept on a relatively short-range scale. Selecting longer range would have allowed the WSO to view the coast for a few minutes as he bore down on it at a speed of almost nine miles a minute. Instead, he had just seconds to examine the coastal radar returns, identify his offset point, update the inertial navigation system, and then turn toward the final attack heading. The earlier update error had been beyond his control, but he may have caught the problem here despite this less than optimal radar technique. In any case, it seems possible that this Aardvark's crew turned toward Tripoli, high on adrenaline and with all systems go, but off course to such an extent that they would be unable to find Qaddafi's headquarters compound. The other possibility is that they were back on course after the turn at the Initial Point (IP), but one final error that would put their bombs well off the target lay ahead.

One of the eighteen attacking aircraft had aborted immediately after being delayed in trying to get its required offload from the tanker. At the end refueling point, the tanker turned north as planned rather than south to help the late attack aircraft. The tankers had been instructed to stay north, out of enemy detection range, and were not aware of the timing problems. The F-111 crew did not direct the tanker south to its advantage and, after leaving the tanker, they realized they could not reach their designated bombing position in time, and had no choice but to call it a night despite the fact that they were flying a perfectly good jet. Some of the other seventeen planes were also encountering difficulties. These included an overheating bleed air system, a faulty generator, a bad infrared target sensor, and another malfunctioning electrical system. Other minor system failures were also registered.

The 48th Wing had been tracking its aircraft and their subsystems by computer since January, keeping a prioritized list of the best jets available at any given moment. Col. Cliff Bingham's award-winning maintenance organization had been told to perform this task without knowing why their hard-driving colonel demanded it. The thirty planes that were used that night were from the top of Cliff's list, but, given just one chance to perform this herculean mission, they broke down more often than we would have expected. Given one hundred chances, my guess is that our planes would have performed better than they did on April 14–15, 1986, over ninety times. But there was to be no second chance.

This assessment does not change the fact that our F-111Fs suffered several critical failures that hurt Operation El Dorado Canyon. But it is too early in this tale to pause to assess the mission's success or failure in relation to F-111F aircraft malfunctions; those subjects will be covered in depth in a later chapter.

The 48th's aircrews were gradually growing more tense as they approached Libya at almost 600 miles an hour. The vast majority, all but a few of the pilots, were on their first combat mission. All the briefings in the world could not prevent their growing anticipation of an experience for which they had been in training for years. Cockpit chatter became more terse and businesslike. The main benefit for many was that their physical discomfort—they had been strapped to their jets for over five hours—was all but forgotten in the accelerating schedule of critical cockpit actions. Captain M. recalls dropping a checklist page and struggling for what seemed like ten minutes to recover it from that inaccessible place where dropped pencils and pages go in jet fighters. Major M. thought that his helmet's earphone speakers had failed—his normally garrulous pilot had been extraordinarily quiet for so long. In every cockpit, pressure grew as they neared Tripoli, waiting for the inevitable, and unpredictable, reaction of the Libyan air defenses. They were correct in believing that Colonel Qaddafi's military was expecting them. The Libyans would have to have been deaf, dumb, and blind not to understand that an attack was imminent.

### FEBRUARY–MARCH 1986

### UNCLOSED LOOPS

While the crews who would fly Operation El Dorado Canyon had continued to treat it as top secret, the international media had had little difficulty in staying abreast of the likelihood of any U.S. military action against Libya. From late January to late March, the probability of a U.S. attack had been low, and the media had reflected this reality in their coverage. As early as January 8, the *New York Times* had reported on "Why Reagan Shuns Force." This was one of several articles that stressed the presence of U.S. citizens in Libya, the potential negative effects of an attack, and the list of peaceful sanctions that could be, and were, substituted for military action. True, an occasional article surfaced stating that the option of military action had not been ruled out: the *Washington Post*'s January 28 piece, "Armed Action Against Libya Still Possible," was an example. But in general, it was understood that an armed attack on Libya was unlikely unless some additional terrorist action occurred which could be directly linked to Colonel Qaddafi or his henchmen.

As peaceful economic sanctions were applied beginning in January, one specific action was included that set the stage for a possible future military response. United States citizens were first asked, and then ordered, to leave Libya. Their removal from the scene finally made the threat of military attack credible.

Even a pseudo air war between the U.S. Navy and the Libyan Air Force in mid-February did not change the picture. Over two dozen air-to-air encounters occurred without a shot being fired on either side. This dangerous fencing happened as Libyan MiG-23 Floggers flew out in response to U.S. Navy exercises north of Qaddafi's unilaterally declared "Line of Death" in the Gulf of Sidra. During similar exercises in January, the colonel himself had sailed toward the U.S. fleet on a Libyan naval patrol boat. This saber-rattling and posturing masked the fact that a direct U.S. military attack was becoming an unrealistic option as the Rome and Vienna tragedies faded into the background.

Others attributed U.S. inaction to more sinister causes. A *Forbes* editorial on February 10 suggested that the Pentagon lacked the ability to conduct a successful military retaliation in a "coherent, decisive way." Citing past failures, Malcolm Forbes, Jr. called the U.S. military establishment "muscle-bound . . . it shuns simplicity and ignores elementary rules of combat." This criticism undoubtedly reflected some level of frustration not only among captains of industry, but also within the American public. Why had we not taken retaliatory action against the sources of terrorism? The average American citizen did not understand.

It was certainly not because the 48th TFW at Lakenheath was not ready. We had been prepared to strike Libya since early January. By February, we were continuing to expand our list of possible targets as various attack options were forwarded from Washington. Eventually, thirty-six targets would be considered, with detailed attack plans built for all but one. The work load involved eventually became too much for the handful of staff officers who had been doing the planning work ever since New Year's Eve. Colonel Westbrook realized it was time to expand the contingency staff when one of those officers, a lieutenant colonel, fell asleep in the wing commander's office while Sam reviewed a draft message the staffer had prepared. Despite security concerns, more of our troops would have to be brought into the top secret process. With their help, the wing stood ready throughout February to execute a small, six-plane raid against any of the multiple targets designated in Libya. Such a raid could be ordered in conjunction with the Navy or independently. It could also occur with or without significant external support from the Navy or other Air Force units. We were prepared for any of these options, but we also saw that it was unlikely that any of them would happen.

With that in mind, a training deployment to Turkey, involving roughly one-fourth of the wing's assets, went ahead on schedule.

While it could have been canceled, the opportunity for expanded training in conjunction with long-distance flights seemed too good to pass up. The 20th Wing at Upper Heyford, England, had been selected for a previous non-stop training mission to Greenland, "Operation Ghost Rider." The 48th had been a candidate as well, but ongoing problems with our aircraft's engines (the F-111Es based at Upper Heyford used a different engine) prevented our involvement. Now we had gained permission from the Turkish Air Force and government to allow us to carry inert heavy ordnance as we flew to our forward NATO base at Incirlik. On February 11, 1986, I flew one of those missions. Our flight of six F-111Fs flew non-stop to Turkey, dropped practice 2,000-pound bombs on the Konya gunnery range, and then landed at Incirlik. The total mission length prior to bomb release was over five hours. We used several similar opportunities, spread over a period of six weeks in February and March, to train our crews and to test our planes. Results were mixed but generally optimistic. By the end of the deployment to Incirlik, we felt confident in our ability to successfully mount a small long-range raid.

With regard to training, it should be noted that, ever since January, the 48th Wing had conducted some specialized training for the few crews (no more than twelve at any one time) who were always on alert for a possible strike against Libya. On the assumption that we would be conducting a small attack at night, overall night training was increased and the selected crews received a larger share of those sorties to help hone their night-flying skills. In addition, on the assumption that at least a few of our targets would be on Libya's Mediterranean coast, some few British coastal towns and areas became targets for a large number of Pave Tack Toss bombing runs during both day and night. I recall only one significant noise complaint after one overzealous crew had pressed home three attacks in twenty minutes against a pastoral coastal village with a radar return that resembled some feature of Tripoli's. This constant but low-key training effort helped maintain a ready force of pilots and WSOs throughout the months that preceded the raid. But, as will be seen later, there was no planned ramp-up from twelve crews to the thirty-plus needed in April. The last-minute decision to triple the size of the 48th's role in the mission forced difficult decisions as to who would or would not fly.

I had returned from Turkey after only one week in order to prepare for Colonel Westbrook's next absence. As a brigadier general-selectee, Sam was slated for "charm school" beginning in late February. This two-week course, conducted in Washington and on various field trips, would apply the final coat of polish to the new Air Force one-stars before they pinned on their rank. Of all the new generals I knew, Sam was the one who least needed the charm treatment.

Of course, Colonel Westbrook would not have been going if El Dorado Canyon had been on the front burner. But at this point there appeared to be no reason why he could not proceed as planned. As a result, he and his wife Kate prepared to return to the United States while I girded myself for another hectic two weeks as the acting wing commander. As things turned out, the fun started early.

On Saturday, February 22, the Westbrooks made a last-minute decision to head for London a day ahead of schedule in order to take in a play and enjoy an evening on the town. Since their flight was scheduled for Sunday morning, their decision had the effect of giving me command for fifteen additional hours.

Everything seemed under control as I retired on Saturday night. But at about 2:30 A.M. on Sunday morning, I was jarred awake by the ring of the redline telephone in my quarters. The command post NCO on the other end of the line said that there had been an attempt to penetrate the base's most secure weapons storage area. Our conversation lasted less than five minutes as I assessed the situation, taking in his answers to my sleepy questions. First and foremost, had they actually gained entry to the high-security area? No—they had been stopped between the final two fences surrounding it. Was the area secure now? Yes. Had all the people involved been found and apprehended? Yes. Had there been any injuries on either side? No. Had the would-be penetrators been identified and, if so, who were they? Yes and no—they were four British females, probably connected with the Campaign for Nuclear Disarmament, the CND, but their names were not yet known. Had the British constabulary and the RAF station commander been informed? Yes—they were on the way to assist in the arrest process. This latter action was necessary since RAF Lakenheath is Her Majesty's territory, and arrests of British citizens can only be made by Her Majesty's representatives.

With these reassuring answers echoing on the line, I hung up knowing that a full report on the incident would be provided the next morning. On other similar occasions, I had leapt out of bed to go to the scene—only to find that there was nothing to see in the pitch-black night. Rather than overreact to an incursion that was apparently over, I returned to bed, agitated but pleased that nothing more serious had happened. To my knowledge, a priority weapons storage area had never before been penetrated. Since the rules allow the use of force to defend that area, it was conceivable that a successful penetration could have resulted in a shooting. I was glad that the British women had not reached a position where that might have been possible. As I was about to drift off to sleep, the redline phone rang again.

The same NCO was on the line, calling to correct one of his previous answers. The weapons area had, in fact, been penetrated. Within seconds after entering the area, the intruders had been confronted by our armed mobile security force, and apprehended. Yes, the incident was certainly over and everything was secure. Now fully awake but not totally reassured, I asked for the wing's chief of security police, Lt. Col. Frank Willingham. In a few minutes, he was on the line, explaining that he had responded to the scene as soon as he understood the situation. He confirmed that things were now in hand, and that extra guards had been posted at the breached fences until repairs could be made in the morning. Satisfied, I asked Frank to meet me in my office with the NCO responsible for weapons storage security at 8 A.M. It was now almost 3:30 A.M.

I gave up any hope of getting more sleep—the gravity of what had happened was sinking in. Somehow, several unarmed women had successfully penetrated one of RAF Lakenheath's most secure areas. Depending on the route they had followed, they had slipped through as many as seven barbed-wire fences to reach their objective. For reasons yet to be explained, the multiple alarm systems on and around those barriers had not prevented their entry. And, finally, they had been confronted by armed American guards in the darkness who, fortunately, had not shot them. That difficult, split-second decision also needed explanation: meeting unknown intruders in the night, why had the guards not opened fire? While concerned about the answer to that question, I was struck by the ominous implications of their other possible decision. Had the guards fired, several British women would likely have been killed or wounded. Luckily, that tragedy had been averted. But that politically explosive scenario haunted me as I awaited the facts.

British fiction and tabloid writers had speculated on this possibility for some time. A play dealing with a conspiracy in which peaceful English demonstrators are killed and then secretly buried on an American airbase had been staged in London. This fictional plot was a sensational, anti-American stretch of the imagination; but a small part of it had almost become fact at Lakenheath on the morning of February 23. Our ongoing preparations for a bombing raid on Libya were no longer our only source of excitement.

Before the 8 A.M. briefing, I talked to Squadron Leader Sharpe, the RAF station commander, about how the British media might react to the night's events. Based on the arrest process he had witnessed and taken part in, Mike's opinion was that the incursion was still ours to handle. No print or broadcast reporters had been in evidence, so he did not expect any national reporting of the incident. His prediction proved correct, with only a brief article in the next day's *East Anglian Times* telling of the break-in. Not counting the wild fictional plots mentioned earlier, that piece was the only publicity that resulted.

Secure in the assumption that we were not about to appear on page one of the *London Times* or the BBC's next broadcast, I waited for the details of what had occurred to emerge at the 8 A.M. meeting. By that time, we would know enough to forward an expanded report up the chain of command—a required message report had been sent within two hours of the incursion, but it was too brief to explain all the pertinent facts. We began the 8 A.M. meeting in the wing commander's office with Frank Willingham and several of his NCOs in attendance.

These were the essential facts they outlined. Four British women, members of the CND, had apparently studied the base for several weeks. Determined to break into the high-security area, they had planned a detailed route that would bring them to the final security fences protecting it with the least chance of observation. Picking a night with little or no moonlight, they reached that point successfully, and began cutting the fences. They skillfully cut through four of them in a matter of seconds. (The reader should note that this was not a matter of poor fences, but of expert, highly practiced fence cutters.) An automatic alarm system had either failed or sounded a delayed alarm, allowing the women to reach the fifth, and final, fence just as the security forces were being alerted. Now entering the glare of a well-lighted area, the women had begun climbing through the hole they had cut in the last fence just as our security forces took their defensive positions. Ignoring orders to halt, they had proceeded toward a weapons storage bunker that, fortunately, was empty. The guard closest to their path had noted that they appeared unarmed, and were carrying signs. When they finally stopped well short of him and began singing, he made the correct decision not to open fire.

Had it happened otherwise, Anglo-American relations could have taken a decided turn for the worse. And it would have been very difficult to second-guess the guard under the circumstances. After all, it was a very dark night and the infiltrators had ignored orders to halt while refusing to identify themselves. In addition, his Air Force training had emphasized weapons proficiency in getting the base security job done. Fortunately, it had also stressed that deadly force should only be used as a last resort. One young airman, isolated in the cold English darkness, had reacted like a real professional. He had assessed the situation and decided not to shoot. But it would have taken very little to change his mind: a few more steps in his direction might have done it. As things turned out, the invading ladies had stopped at an empty weapons igloo, allowing time for a brief standoff during which the fully alerted security forces could decide on how to proceed. The fact that the women were singing songs in English while sitting on the spotlighted grass—unlikely acts for terrorists bent on death and destruction—undoubtedly helped save their lives. After a few minutes of prudent assessment, the NCO in charge of the scene decided to arrest them. This was done without incident.

With a fairly complete picture of the night's events now available, it was time to close the loop with Major General McInerney at Mildenhall. His headquarters had been addressed in our early morning message report, so he undoubtedly knew of the incursion—now he would receive the details.

Our first attempt to call the general found him away from his quarters: he and his family were attending church. I dismissed the idea of interrupting the religious service; it seemed unnecessary and overly dramatic since his notification and departure from the chapel would cause a stir. A second attempt to reach him was also unsuccessful; services were still in progress. I left a message with the operator to let me know as soon as the general was available.

By this time, about 10:30 on Sunday morning, our phones at the 48th were beginning to ring as higher headquarters sought details not included in our message of the wee hours. One of those inquiries, from USAFE headquarters at Ramstein, went directly to Major General McInerney. As fate would have it, this was the first call to reach him after he left the chapel. It was also his first indication that anything unusual had happened at Lakenheath—his staff had apparently not told him of our earlier message.

Information is an important commodity in any power relationship. On Sunday morning, February 23, my failure to close the loop with McInerney had placed him in an embarrassing position vis-à-vis his boss, General Donnelly. Donnelly's apparent knowledge of the break-in at Lakenheath before McInerney knew of it could be considered a threat. And it seemed likely that, as far as McInerney was concerned, it was once again my fault that he had not been informed in a timely manner. As in January, he had been left exposed.

The general called at about 11 A.M. When would it be convenient for me to brief him on the incident at Lakenheath? At his convenience, of course. Within hours, we had met and he had been briefed on the facts listed here. He agreed that a detailed investigation was appropriate, and concurred with our decision to conduct it internally—disasters require external review; near disasters do not. We conducted an investigation that bluntly assessed our security system, our security forces, their weapons, and their state of training. This report was not dictated by any regulation or order from above. Nevertheless, it reached wide-ranging conclusions applicable to security issues throughout the Air Force. Third Air Force concurred with the report after minor modification, and it was then sent to USAFE. There is some hope that it has served as a catalyst for needed changes.

Our report reached Ramstein in early March. Sam Westbrook reviewed it upon returning to Lakenheath from Washington on March 8. I understood his basic reaction: he was thankful that he had gone to the theater on February 22. After spending just six days in England, he took advantage of the lull in Operation El Dorado Canyon to travel to Turkey to supervise the continuing training there. Almost immediately after Sam's departure, and much to our surprise, the contingency heated up. And once again, as in the February 23 incident described above, we failed to close a loop.

On Sunday, March 16, a message arrived tasking the 48th to build attack plans for several new targets. That message also ordered that a briefing about the new plans be given to General Donnelly at Ramstein on Wednesday, March 19. The extent of the tasks dictated that this briefing could not be completed until some time on Tuesday afternoon. Without giving details over an unsecure line, I called Major General McInerney Monday morning to invite him to an "update briefing on new activity regarding our current tasking"—he had not been an addressee on the Sunday message. He agreed to join us at Lakenheath on Tuesday afternoon, perfect timing in relation to our plan to complete our briefing for the CINC and then fly the briefing officers to Germany. All seemed well as Tuesday morning dawned: for once, the Third Air Force commander would be fully informed on our new contingency plans before the information reached his boss.

But at this point, Murphy's Law went into operation. By mid-morning on Tuesday, we had caught wind of a rumor that McInerney would not be coming to Lakenheath as scheduled—he had decided to visit RAF Alconbury forty miles to the west where the 10th Tactical Reconnaissance Wing was preparing for a change of command. A few quick calls confirmed the rumor: the general was en route to Alconbury and would not return until well after

5 P.M. The T-39 executive jet taking our officers to Germany was leaving at 5:15 P.M. Mighty efforts to either get the general to Lakenheath earlier or to delay the plane carrying the briefers were equally unsuccessful. McInerney finally called to find out what was up at around 5:45 P.M., when the briefers and the briefing were already flying to the continent. An offer to give him an immediate update on what they were carrying was rejected; instead, the general would receive the briefing in his office the next morning.

I knew I had screwed up. Somehow, the importance of the Tuesday afternoon briefing had not been adequately conveyed to the general. Accordingly, he had considered it routine and had canceled it without a second thought. We had again failed to close the loop, and the general's confidence in the 48th Wing's on-scene leadership had received another jolt. I understood all this when on Wednesday morning, March 19, we drove to Mildenhall to brief McInerney on attack plans which General Donnelly had seen in Germany ninety minutes earlier. The general was not amused. And, by then, the author was more than a little intimidated.

After watching my embarrassment over the course of the half-hour briefing, McInerney dismissed the other 48th officers so that we could speak privately. Once we were alone, he explained the important role of Third Air Force in this contingency. It all tied in with Numbered Air Force (NAF) Enhancement, a management initiative which was supposed to increase the role, and the clout, of these support commands in day-to-day operations. He emphasized that he should have been kept informed at any cost, using all means available, to ensure that he was able to make an input to the planning process. While he had no major disagreement with the plans we had built, he was not pleased that they had reached USAFE without his review. Did I understand? I said "yessir," but the real answer was "not entirely." I certainly understood his clear anger over being bypassed again, albeit inadvertently, by the 48th Wing. But if his role was critical, why was the general not even receiving messages regarding El Dorado Canyon?

In retrospect, I believe he needed to make this point to the CINC, General Donnelly, and to the Deputy Chief of Staff for

Operations Maj. Gen. David Forgan at Ramstein. Beginning in January, Major General Forgan had been given nominal control over the Air Force part of the contingency by Donnelly. The short secure chain of command from Ramstein to Lakenheath caused friction as it systematically excluded Third Air Force and its commander. As the contingency developed, all of the principal players in its execution happened to be stationed in or operating from England, Third Air Force's one and only area of interest. Problems were inevitable. When it appeared that the mission would not be flown—over ninety percent of the time—Third Air Force could be actively involved. Since the mission was so unlikely to occur, it was probably thought that fine-tuning of the battle plans was not inappropriate; it showed both interest and involvement per NAF Enhancement. During the brief periods when the mission seemed likely to go, the imperative for headquarters involvement was even greater.

When and if problems occurred, all involved wanted to know what had caused them. Excuses for missteps on earlier contingencies in and around Lebanon had been weak—if things went wrong on this mission, no one wanted to be in the position of having to claim ignorance. So while the wing did almost all of the nuts-and-bolts planning for the thirty-plus targets, our efforts received exhaustive reviews at all higher headquarters. Their input led to improvement to the basic plans, but simultaneously caused a significant increase in the wing's work load.

The question of the chain of command for the contingency came up only once between January and April. In a private discussion with Major General Forgan in his office at Ramstein, he had asked me if the 48th needed McInerney "out of [our] hair." My answer was that I did not believe that was possible or desirable; what was needed was a complete understanding by all the players as to who was in charge: USAFE/DO or 3 AF/CC? Perhaps Forgan could take it up with Generals Donnelly and McInerney for resolution. While I understand that a closed door meeting among the three generals did occur, it appears that this sticky problem was not conclusively resolved. Had everyone known that the mission was going to happen, it is nearly certain that the chain of command would have been set in concrete at some point. Instead, the century's most improbable Air Force mission remained in partial control of many far-flung hands until the very end. Fortunately, the hands with the ultimate responsibility, those of the pilots and WSOs on the F-111 sticks, did superior work. The success of the Air Force part of the mission, despite the multilevel command structure, was largely due to the crews' efforts.

The phrase "Air Force part of the mission" requires further clarification at this point. Operation El Dorado Canyon, as stated earlier, was a joint mission involving two naval air wings from the carriers *America* and *Coral Sea*. In fact, El Dorado Canyon was under the overall command of Vice Adm. Frank Kelso, then commander of the Sixth Fleet based in the Mediterranean. Admiral Kelso's headquarters aboard the *America* served as the single focus for command decisions and interservice coordination for the mission. In addition to conducting the entire strike in eastern Libya against targets in the area of Benghazi, planes from both carriers supported the Air Force attack against heavily defended Tripoli. While more will be said later about the particular Navy support provided near Tripoli, details of the Navy's raid in eastern Libya remain beyond the scope of this book.

At various times between January and April, the odds varied as to whether an attack on Libya would be a Navy-only, Air Force–only, or joint mission. When the tea leaves said "joint," appropriate planning initiatives were taken to ensure that there would be no interservice foul-ups. One of the 48th's most competent lieutenant colonels spent weeks on the *America*, coordinating details with the naval aviators and fleet defenders. His intermittent presence there helped relieve one of our greatest fears: the possibility that F-111s would be shot down by the air defense system of the U.S. Sixth Fleet. Gradually, we gained confidence that the procedures to prevent fratricide would probably work. Nevertheless, it was not until March that this concern was pushed into the background.

The presence of KC-10 tankers in England during March gave rise to what turned out to be a practice mission involving all of the key players that would be involved in the actual raid. Major General Forgan, Colonel Westbrook, and the author were among several officers who flew onboard a KC-10 mother ship, refueling both F-111Fs from Lakenheath and EF-111s from Upper Heyford. Unlike the real mission, this small-scale rehearsal took us across France to the mid-Mediterranean where our jets "bombed" a Sixth Fleet ship simulating a target. They egressed to the north, practicing the communications and flight procedures that would ensure their safety from any Navy "friendly fire." The small attack force then rejoined the KC-10 and returned to its bases in the United Kingdom. This six-hour mission proved the viability of the joint communications that would be used on the raid, and built confidence that the two services could do the job together. The flight was primarily a Third Air Force idea, and contributed significantly to the smooth interaction between the services in April. It should also be noted that it took place well before the expanded joint plan for the raid had been finalized. In this instance, Major General McInerney and his staff certainly deserve congratulations for their foresight.

As the end of March approached, the Navy began independent operations north of Libya. Ordered to conduct Freedom of Navigation exercises in the international waters of the Gulf of Sidra, the Sixth Fleet sent surface combatants and warplanes into the area for a period lasting more than three days. From March 22 to March 26, the Libyan reaction was consistently aggressive, beginning with the firing of SA-5 missiles at the Navy jets. The U.S. Navy's response included the destruction of Libyan guided missile patrol boats and an attack on the offending SA-5 site at Sirte. By the time "Operation Prairie Fire" ended, at least two Libyan patrol boats had been sunk by missiles and cluster bombs, and several others were reportedly damaged. The Libyan SA-5 radars had also been temporarily put out of commission by anti-radiation missiles. As the situation quieted on March 27, it appeared that Libya had been properly chastised for its illegal military action in international waters. All U.S. Navy reactions had been in retaliation for aggressive Libyan acts, and the amount of force used had been measured. There seemed to be no justification for any further military action against Libya based on Operation Prairie Fire. Other unspecified things would have to occur to trigger an airstrike. On April 2, 1986, they began to happen.

That morning, TWA Flight 840 en route from Rome to Athens had just begun its descent, when a bomb exploded in the passenger cabin. The blast ripped a hole in the fuselage through which four people, all Americans, were sucked to their deaths. Among the four were a young Greek-born American mother and her infant daughter. Three of the four were later determined to have been alive when they struck the ground after falling nearly three miles.[1]

While the investigation of these murders quickly found evidence connecting the bombing to various obscure Palestinian and pro-Syrian splinter groups, there was no direct proof of Libyan involvement. By itself, the terrorist bombing of the TWA plane on April 2 might not have caused a military response against Colonel Qaddafi. But, with U.S. outrage over this crime still fresh, a second fatal incident occurred which would trigger the bombing of Libya.

Near 2 A.M. on the morning of April 5, 1986, another bomb wreaked havoc in the popular La Belle Disco in West Berlin. Planted in a restroom near the main dance floor, the device instantly killed one American soldier and a Turkish woman; a second U.S. GI would later die of his wounds. Hundreds of others, mostly Americans, were injured by the blast.[2]

The question of whether or not Libya was responsible for the blast has been a matter of serious debate ever since that night. That responsibility has been disputed by a number of experts in various publications, but has also been supported elsewhere by equally authoritative sources. In any case, in 1990, in the midst of the turmoil surrounding the reunification of Germany, reports surfaced from East German defectors confirming the fact that the attack had been carried out by the Libyan People's Bureau in East Berlin. Lending credence to their accounts were details such as the fact that high officials of the East German government knew of the planned attack in advance. Contemporary accounts that now seem to be at least partially confirmed by the East German defectors included the following information: the bombing had been preceded by the interception of a message from the Libyan People's Bureau in East Berlin to Tripoli which predicted an imminent "joyous event." U.S. and allied commanders took this to be warning of a possible terrorist action. Despite efforts to warn U.S. personnel at several known hangouts, the bomb went off before it could be found or the disco could be evacuated. Shortly after the explosion, a second monitored message from

East Berlin to Tripoli claimed that the event had been successfully completed. It supposedly also said that the event could not
be traced to the People's Bureau. At last, a smoking gun had
been found with Colonel Qaddafi's fingerprints still on it. The
conditions to prompt the execution of a retaliatory strike on Libya
had finally been met. But, it would take several additional days
for the details that would allow participation by U.S. F-111s
based in Britain to be sorted out. Gaining permission from Mrs.
Thatcher's government would be one hurdle. Getting French approval to overfly their terrorism-ridden nation would be another.
As things developed, President Reagan was only fifty percent successful in his effort.

# SIX

# ATTACK

Three separate lines of F-111Fs were bearing down on Tripoli as the clock approached midnight, Greenwich mean time. Identified by radio call signs, the attacking elements (each planned to include three aircraft) were "Remit," "Elton," and "Karma" aimed at Qaddafi's headquarters at Azziziyah Barracks; "Jewel" targeted against the Sidi Balal terrorist training camp; and "Puffy" and "Lujac" assigned to the Tripoli airport. Simultaneously, supporting Navy and Air Force aircraft were approaching their preplanned positions, from which they would engage the Libyan defenses around Tripoli. In eastern Libya, a similarly coordinated, all-Navy effort was underway. In addition, both attack forces were being "CAPped" by Combat Air Patrols of Navy F-14 fighters—all aircraft heading north after the raid toward the carriers *America* and *Coral Sea* would pass muster as friendlies or be shot down.

Ideally, it would have been best if the three Tripoli area targets could have all been struck simultaneously. Theoretically, the total time in the target area could have been reduced to less than five or six minutes while still providing an adequate margin of safety. But the late change that tripled the raid's size had not allowed sufficient time to accomplish that. Instead, an old January attack plan for the Tripoli airport had been meshed with an intermediate March plan for Sidi Balal, and both had been tied to a brand-new April plan for Qaddafi's headquarters. All three plans had been further changed and polished during the final forty-eight hours before takeoff when the numbers of aircraft per target had at last been finalized. The result was a less-than-ideal but workable compromise that hit all three targets in a reasonable length of time—all Lakenheath F-111Fs would be on and off target in less than eleven minutes.

Lieutenant Colonel F., the pilot of "Remit-31," looked through his windscreen as the bright lights of Tripoli became more distinct. His bombs would be the first to drop on what appeared to be a surprisingly active city at 2 A.M. He concentrated on keeping up his airspeed so that the line of eight other F-111Fs would not overrun his; with a minimum of thirty seconds' spacing between aircraft, precise timing control was critical. That spacing depended on the target, with the use of displaced aiming points and divergent attack headings increasing the separation at the airport target to up to seventy-five seconds. Each aircraft was on its own at this point, trying to ensure that it was at the time and place required. Like all the others, Lieutenant Colonel F. had no idea whether or not anybody else was where they were supposed to be. In fact, as he closed on the target at over nine miles a minute, the number of jets behind him had already been reduced; still others were rapidly falling out as various aircraft problems developed. At this point, Lieutenant Colonel F. had too much on his mind to worry about the others; they would have to take care of themselves. He heaved a small sigh of relief when he saw a Navy aircraft fire an anti-radiation missile at the Libyan radars—at least the defense suppression package was on station and doing its job. Roughly thirty seconds remained until the pull-up point for his Pave Tack Toss maneuver. Downtown Tripoli was at twelve o'clock, level, less than ten miles ahead.[1]

About twenty-five miles in trail, Major S. was also bearing down on Tripoli as the seventh aircraft in the long line attacking the Azziziyah Barracks complex. He too was unaware of the position and status of the others in the line, but he had more reason to be concerned. One of the crews up ahead was supposed to give him an assessment of the Libyan defenses if possible. Major S. needed the information to comply with an unusual request he had received before takeoff. For reasons about to be explained, he had been told by the Third Air Force commander to abort his flight's attack if the Libyan defenses appeared too formidable;

the assumption seemed to be that his previous combat experience would allow him to successfully make this call. His decision could reduce the attack on Qaddafi's headquarters by one-third, dropping the final three F-111s from the picture. Major S. was taken aback by the suggestion. "Here they were asking me to fly six thousand miles with the possibility of aborting my flight because of threat reaction." He had never been given such an option in seventy-six combat missions in Southeast Asia. Moreover, Air Force training, for obvious reasons, does not concentrate on subjective assessments of enemy defenses as a reason for going home early. On the contrary, as the famous song suggests, "Nothing can stop the U.S. Air Force!"

In an attempt to comply with the general's request, Major S. had sought out Lieutenant Colonel A. the night before. Since A. would be ninety seconds ahead of him in the line, would he call back if the target-area defenses proved especially heavy? A.'s reply was a half-hearted "yes"—he did not understand the question nor what the major could possibly do with the information. The major was just as confused by the situation; even if Lieutenant Colonel A.'s warning call came through, the decision was still supposed to be his and he would have only seconds to make it. Major S.'s thoughts of his dilemma were interrupted by a flash on the horizon—the first bombs had landed on Azziziyah. A second series of flashes followed shortly—they seemed to get bigger and brighter as his jet closed rapidly on the target. But surprisingly no additional explosions were seen: he had expected bomb flashes every thirty seconds. After the second set of bombs went off, no others appeared. The significance of this puzzling lack of bomb impacts was not instantly apparent in "Karma-51"'s busy cockpit. Had Major S. had time to mull it over, he would have realized that the jets in front of him were either not dropping their bombs or, worse, were not there at all. The latter was the case for Lieutenant Colonel A., the man who was to have assessed the defenses. A major malfunction had caused him to abort his bomb run just before reaching Tripoli: no warning call of any sort would be forthcoming.

The defenses of course were anything but asleep and unprepared. Intelligence briefings that suggested they would be at home in bed after midnight were sorely mistaken. Despite the fact that it was 2 A.M. in Libya, the Libyan SAMs and Triple-A were just waiting for something to shoot at. After over three months of explicit saber-rattling and several days of mounting worldwide expectation of a U.S. attack, the Libyan military would have been criminally negligent if they had not been on alert. The only factor that cut the 48th Wing's losses was that the SAM operators and Triple-A gunners did not seem to know the specific details of the raid's plans. But they were certainly ready to shoot back.

Lieutenant Colonel F. discovered that in the middle of his Pave Tack Toss maneuver against Qaddafi's house and headquarters. As the first in line, he had had the luxury of making his bombing run before the defenders became fully alert. Nevertheless, he was surprised to find a stream of 23 mm tracers smoothly tracking his escape maneuver—fortunately the stream bent back and passed behind him as the gunners failed to adequately compensate for his high speed. He pulled a bit harder so that he could get to the egress heading quicker, a control input that caused the Aardvark's tail to obscure the laser designator a split-second prior to bomb impact. In the right seat, Captain H. saw the bombs hit immediately after the target disappeared, and his impression was that they had covered the target. Actually, the bombs had landed fifty feet short of the residence, but even this near miss had done considerable damage. In addition to the structural damage to the building and the casualties inside, these bombs had partially destroyed Qaddafi's nearby tent. His shell-shocked appearance when he reappeared weeks after the raid would fuel speculation that he had been in the tent. If this was true, his injuries were largely a matter of chance—his whereabouts were unknown to us as we finished our planning, and the tent had never been included as a specific aiming point. (The issue of Colonel Qaddafi as a target of the raid is not as simple as the preceding statements may imply. For that reason, it will be addressed in detail in a later chapter.)

The crew of "Remit-31" had completed their attack successfully, but not without opposition. In addition to some beeps and whistles from the radar warning equipment, indicating SAM activity, the *first* attacking F-111F had been shot at by radar-aimed

Triple-A at 2 A.M. Libyan time! The months of forewarning had not been lost on the Libyans; the implications for the rest of the U.S. fighter bombers were ominous.

If any doubt remained that the U.S. blow had been telegraphed, it disappeared the next morning. On April 15, the *New York Times* edition published within hours of the raid included a front page report from Edward Schumacher in Tripoli. Laid out side by side with the first stories of the actual bombing, it detailed the Libyan preparations that had been visible during the final day prior to the mission. Libyan actions had included establishing a twenty-four-hour alert for hospital staffs, dispersing warplanes at airfields around Tripoli to make them more difficult targets, and moving mobile SAM and Triple-A air defense batteries to new locations.

Those redeployed defenses had become more active thirty seconds later as Captain B. followed "Remit-31" down the chute. The sky was now filling with man-made objects, most designed to kill F-111s. Libyan SAMs were being launched from multiple sites, each leaving its distinctive visual and sometimes electronic signature. Flares sent up from boats in the Tripoli harbor illuminated the entire scene, turning night into near daylight. Not that the F-111s could not be seen without flares; most were being forced to use at least some afterburner to keep their speed high enough. The thirty-foot sheets of flame coming from their tails served as excellent aim points for the Libyan gunners. The volume and rate of fire of the Triple-A increased as the attack progressed; fortunately, none of the flak hit the attacking aircraft. But the crew of "Remit-32" had other difficulties that made their attack unsuccessful. Due primarily to equipment failure, the second raider reached the position to perform the toss maneuver just as the crew realized that they were not lined up on the correct aim point. The aborted toss bomb maneuver turned into a decision to retain the 2,000-pound bombs through a night, low-level, high-speed pass over downtown Tripoli. This pylon turn was only possible because the Libyan flares provided enough light to allow the pilot to safely fly the maneuver manually. Later, the bombs would be jettisoned at sea.

Thirty more seconds put "Remit-33" into the heart of the gauntlet, and, despite a radar altimeter problem and a faulty lamp on the Pave Tack pod, the crew felt that conditions looked good for their bomb delivery. Many SAMs were in the air but Captain J. did not have time to worry about them due to the tremendous volume of Triple-A. In the right seat, Captain H. watched the flak get worse and urged Captain J. not to use any more afterburner. He was convinced that the barrage fire would quickly become even deadlier aimed fire if they lit their burners one more time. Captain J. agreed, and Captain H. lowered his head into his scopes and tried to ignore the fascinating fireworks display they were flying through. The tracers seemed to be criss-crossing above them as they approached their pull-up for the toss, but it appeared that they would be in the middle of the flak at the top of the toss maneuver. Captain J. recalls a feeling of total vulnerability and imminent destruction. He also remembers a by-the-book Pave Tack Toss pull-up, and a weapons release at the nominal position that would put the LGBs in the basket neces-sary to allow final laser guidance. But, in the twenty-two seconds that the bombs were falling, the Pave Tack video picture did not "cue up" to the target, and Captain H. in the right seat could not find the aim point. As a result, the four 2,000-pound LGBs fell ballistically, landing without laser guidance within a few hundred feet of the designated target. Post-flight review of the cockpit videotape showed that the target was indeed within the field of view, but that it was almost entirely obscured by the smoke from "Remit-31"'s bombs. The same video also showed two short-range, Soviet-built SAMs rising from a location not predicted by intelligence sources. But the missiles and the flak soon fell behind and the crew was overcome by a feeling of vast relief as they flew out of range of the shore-based defenses.

"Remit-33"'s close miss was at least partly attributable to the unforecast headwinds that blew smoke and debris to positions that interfered with the later attackers. The stiff wind played havoc with the Tripoli raiders throughout the brief attack, forcing the use of afterburner to maintain planned ground speeds and effec-tively hiding targets on a random basis from all but the first planes. "Remit-33" had followed the ROE with a basically good jet, but had been victimized by a balky Pave Tack system and by their leader's smoke. Nevertheless, 33's bombs did hit in the tar-get complex and caused no collateral damage. Others would not be as fortunate.

Looking ahead, Major S. in "Karma-51" saw the impacts of the bombs from "Remit-31" and "Remit-33." He was also closely monitoring the defensive activity they encountered. Not that he could concentrate on any one thing; the cockpit demands were too great to allow that. Like many of the other attackers, he was beginning to have problems with his automatic terrain-following system. It would not hold altitude and, instead, was commanding "fly-ups," emergency climb maneuvers, for no obvious reason. He "paddled off" the system using a safety interrupt switch on the stick, and continued to the target, flying manually. Speed and altitude control required intense concentration, and concerns about the Triple-A display ahead caused an impromptu decision regarding use of his engines' afterburners. Rather than provide the long trails of fire as aiming points, he would cease afterburner operation two minutes out from the target. The trick worked and caused "Karma-51" to be only about five seconds late.

But reducing the jet's visual signature only fixed one part of the problem; radar-guided SAMs and Triple-A did not have to "see" you to shoot you down. Major S. was struck by the volume and variety of SAM fire; Southeast Asia had been a one-SAM war using the now obsolete SA-2 Guideline missile. The Libyan defenses included Soviet-built improved SA-2s and newer SA-3s, SA-6s, SA-8s, as well as French-made Crotales. With the exception of the SA-5s which were too far away, it seemed that all of the missiles named were in the air. Fortunately, most if not all appeared to be unguided—the defense suppression forces using electronic jamming and Anti-Radiation Missiles, ARMs, known as either Shrikes or HARMs, were having their effect. Major S. was impressed by the spectacular show put on by both the enemy's missiles and by the U.S. ARMs. The Crotale looked like a Fourth of July bottle rocket; with a large flash, bright-but-brief streak of flame, and the suspenseful wait for the warhead to function. Two friendly Shrikes flashed overhead with great sheets of distinctive blue flame that distracted the Aardvark crew as they fought to stay on course, on altitude, and on speed.

Major S. listened closely, waiting for some word from Lieutenant Colonel A. who was supposed to be ahead. When the silence on his radio made it obvious that no outside threat assessment was available, he made one himself. Should he abort his formation? Were the defenses ahead too hot? The flak looked lighter compared to Hanoi, but the SAMs looked a lot tougher. The good news was that the SAMs did not appear to be guiding. His decision, made in seconds, was to press on. What he could not know was that time was improving the performance of the Libyan SAM operators. A post-raid assessment of his mission tape showed clearly that a Libyan SAM had locked on to "Karma-51." If his comment ("Turns out, I was the only one on the raid to get locked up by one of the SAMs") is limited to the raid's survivors, it is probably accurate. If it includes "Karma-52," manned by Captains Ribas-Dominicci and Lorence and less than one minute behind Major S., it is probably mistaken.

No one will ever know for certain what happened in "Karma-52"'s cockpit. There has been much speculation about what caused the aircraft to crash, with a lot of initial support for the theory that the pilot simply flew his jet into the water. Among those reported to believe that theorem have been various Air Force and Pentagon spokesmen, unnamed defense industry executives, and ex-secretary of the Navy, John F. Lehman, Jr. Indeed, in the immediate wake of the mission, the pilot error theory seemed reasonable based on all the known facts. Crews were being forced to fly their aircraft manually at low altitude and high speed at night—their automatic systems were malfunctioning. Crews were distracted by the Libyan flares and the heavy Triple-A and SAM fire. Finally, this crew was one of many on their first combat mission; their performance was open to review based on the known effects of hostile fire on those in combat for the first time.

Other theories were voiced but drew less support. The authoritative aviation magazine, *Aviation Week & Space Technology*, fed speculation when its April 4, 1988, issue reported that "one of the F-111's own weapons exploded, causing it to crash 6 mi. prior to reaching the Libyan coast and *out of range of Libyan defenses*." (Emphasis added.) To this author's knowledge, there is no evidence whatsoever to support the theory of "Karma-52" being destroyed by its own weapons. In early 1989, a senior Air Force electronics expert suggested that electromagnetic interference (EMI) may have caused the jet to crash.[2] His unsupported suggestion drew criticism from the Pentagon when it was published early that year. As Pentagon spokesmen correctly noted, there was no substantive evidence to support the stated conclusion. That same spokesman, as reported in the February 13, 1989, issue of *Air Force Times*, suggested that, "at this point, there is insufficient information to determine exactly what caused the loss of that F-111." While the service spokesman was correct in his statement—the exact cause of the destruction of "Karma-52" may never be known—he was nevertheless unaware that new information had just become available which strongly argued against some of the existing theories.

The new information referred to was in the results of the January 1989 autopsy performed on the returned body of Maj. (posthumously promoted) Fernando Ribas-Dominicci. There will be more on Fernando's return later in these pages, but for now it is sufficient to give the autopsy's primary conclusion: his death was due to drowning. He had suffered no fractures. He had no internal injuries.

Even these striking facts do not entirely rule out the pilot error theory. Other F-111 crashes at sea have involved crewmen who survived the initial impact only to drown. In addition, the autopsy did show that Fernando had suffered some impact-type injuries. Therefore, is there any reason not to believe the original post-mission theory that the pilot accidentally flew into the Mediterranean?

In the author's estimation, the answer is a resounding yes. First of all, the other F-111 crashes referred to occurred in peacetime at much lower airspeeds and without live ordnance aboard the aircraft. Both the higher combat airspeed and the weapons load of "Karma-52" make it less likely that either crewman could have survived flying into the Med without massive physical trauma. What then caused Major Ribas-Dominicci's impact injuries? The most likely explanation appears to be that they were produced by the shock of *the F-111's ejection capsule* striking the water before full deployment of its parachutes. I believe that Fernando Ribas-Dominicci and Paul Lorence ejected from their crippled Aardvark an instant before it crashed into the Mediterranean, but at an altitude and attitude which prevented their capsule escape system from fully functioning.

Why did they bail out? The only reasonable conclusion is that their aircraft was disabled and perhaps out of control. What was the most likely cause for a "must eject" situation developing at that point in the mission? The theory that their own weapons exploded appears extremely improbable—such failures are very, very rare; and if it was going to occur, it would likely have happened much earlier in their six-hour flight. In addition, a successful ejection from low altitude after a 2,000-pound bomb exploded fifteen feet behind the cockpit is very hard to envision. The EMI theory seems more credible, but still highly improbable. If the aircraft went out of control due to the "electronic blizzard"[3] it encountered, it would have been likely to pitch either up or down. Up would have been no real problem—abort the bomb run, regain control as airspeed decays from 550-plus knots, and return to base. Down would have had immediate, fatal results—ejection would be highly improbable due to the reaction times involved.

That leaves the unsurprising and very believable theory that "Karma-52" was shot down. After all, this was a combat mission into thoroughly alerted and capable air defenses—the most technically sophisticated air defenses yet encountered by American air power. Those defenses had been adjusted and fine-tuned to deal with a possible U.S. attack for over three months. They reacted, at 2 A.M. to the very first attacking aircraft, and responded with measures such as flares that must have been deployed specifically to counter tactics that they or their advisors had read about in a variety of open sources. As Admiral Kelso, the Sixth Fleet's commander, said after the raid, "[nobody] has ever flown a mission in any more dense SAM environment than they were in."[4] The volume of both Triple-A and SAMs increased as the later attackers approached, and the aircraft immediately ahead of the plane that was destroyed was the only surviving jet to be successfully tracked by a SAM. Moreover, "Karma-52" had flown what appeared to be a good jet for over six hours prior to going down. And, finally, despite *Aviation Week's* contention, Fernando and Paul were apparently well within range of some longer-reaching Libyan SAMs like the SA-3. With all this in mind, what is a likely scenario for "Karma-52"'s destruction?

Perhaps the pilot error theory deserves a final look. Is there any chance whatsoever that F-111F Number 70-2389 was just flown into the sea? Since nothing in aviation is beyond the realm of possibility, the answer is yes—there is that chance. But several crucial pieces of evidence seem to rule it out. They include the accounts of several eyewitnesses, the autopsy results, and the fact that the aircraft immediately ahead was tracked by a SAM.

Based on that evidence, it seems sound to suggest that "Karma-52" was shot down by a Libyan SAM. Despite the various measures designed to counter those systems, including defensive equipment aboard their own aircraft, this particular SAM got through, exploding near enough to disable Fernando and Paul's jet. Various eyewitnesses disagree as to whether the fireball from the Aardvark appeared on the water or in the air—some Navy aviators saw it descend several hundred feet before hitting the water. At least one crewman of the "Jewel" element, flying behind and to the right of "Karma," reported the fireball as being ahead, to the left, and slightly *above* his altitude. I now credit those accounts as accurate: Fernando and Paul were hit, caught fire, lost control, and ejected. All of this occurred so quickly that their ejection was too late—the slowing capsule smashed into the water before its parachutes could fully deploy. The impact probably rendered both men unconscious, and they subsequently drowned.

Even if they had somehow remained conscious at water entry, it would have been unlikely that they could have survived. In the dark, shocked and confused, with a capsule that was probably sinking after suffering major damage, it would have been a miracle if either man had been able to safely evacuate. The final result would have been the same: death by drowning. Whatever the exact circumstances of their final moments in the Mediterranean, the fact remained that "Karma-52"'s crewmen had come a long way on their first and final combat mission. Flying in a tactically untenable position within the El Dorado Canyon attack force, they had almost reached their target despite the defenses. What is sad is that they should never have been ordered to fly in that position in the first place.

As the destruction of "Karma-52" was occurring, the other major drama of the operation was taking place almost simultaneously. With everything looking good in both the left and right seats, "Karma-51" had reached the point in the attack where the four 2,000-pound LGBs had been released. But in the seconds prior to bomb release, the pilot and WSO had both recognized that something was wrong. The pilot noted that the bombs took a few more seconds to automatically release than had been expected—he was just about to call for backup manual release when the computer finally found a solution and dropped the weapons. The WSO searched the infrared display of Tripoli for the specific target in the Azziziyah Barracks compound, but nothing looked right. Unable to find his target, he had no choice but to let the bombs fall ballistically; the Laser Guidance System is useless unless the target can be identified and tracked by the crew. The 8,000 pounds of destruction dropped to where fate and gravity had pointed them—to a populated area of downtown Tripoli, very close to the French embassy. The resulting casualties among innocent civilians constituted the unfortunate "collateral damage" that we had tried so hard to avoid. Despite those efforts, some single error or combination of errors had caused those bombs to go astray.

High-speed refueling, unplanned course adjustments to make up time, bad offset aim point coordinates, and less-than-optimal radar techniques: these were all factors that may have contributed to "Karma-52"'s errant bombs. But the possibility remains that, despite all these problems, the plane was still on course and headed for its target until one last error occurred. It has been suggested that the wrong offset position was inadvertently selected. The computer, believing that the aim point selected was at another location, dutifully directed the aircraft to a point where the total bombing error was nearly one and a half miles. The LGBs dropped long, and the results made worldwide headlines. No one in the 48th felt good about that result, least of all the crew that released the bombs. They can take comfort in the fact that they were not the first aircrew to commit such an error, and they will certainly not be the last. Indeed, many of their contemporaries discovered that fact during 1991's Desert Storm. In most cases, though, they avoided the glare of international publicity and condemnation that briefly followed El Dorado Canyon.

The huge fireball that had been "Karma-52" quickly subsided

as the three F-111Fs, call sign "Jewel," assigned to the Sidi Balal terrorist training camp began their attacks. Their course roughly paralleled that of the nine preceding jets, but the location of their target (a few miles west of downtown Tripoli) prevented them from having to run the full gauntlet of Libyan defenses. When the winds at the target proved to be significantly different from those forecast, even this small force encountered problems of smoke and debris from one aircraft's bombs obscuring the target for another.

The crew of the third aircraft of the element, "Jewel-63," was surprised to encounter this problem. After the bombs were released, the pilot, another Captain J., had listened as his exuberant WSO, Captain C., spontaneously talked the LGBs toward the target. In the process, he made the raid's only quotable comment, "This one's for you, Colonel [Qaddafi]!" But just before the LGBs could find their target, smoke from the earlier explosions of bombs from "Jewel-61" interfered with the laser guidance, causing 63's bombs to miss by a few dozen yards. As at Azziziyah, damage was done, but not to the extent expected of precision bombing. Fortunately for the three aircraft of the "Jewel" element, the defenses that engaged them seemed slightly less intense than they had been a few minutes earlier; the shift of the attack away from downtown Tripoli had added to the "Fog of War" and seemed to cause the Libyans to relax momentarily.

Meanwhile, the final six-plane attack force was closing in on its target: the military side of the Tripoli airport. The "Puffy" and "Lujac" elements prosecuting this attack had been among the first to take off and would be the last to land. Their attack plan, devised early in the contingency as one of the first options considered, involved a long overland approach to the target which served to bypass the main body of Libyan defenses facing the sea.

The overland part of their flight plan required these six F-111s to fully utilize their automatic terrain-following radar systems in modes that the other elements did not need. It also added an element of stress to their mission that was not present for those attacking from the sea. The best explanation of this is that the sea is basically level under most weather conditions; its altitude is a known. The Libyan terrain, on the other hand, was irregular and to some extent unknown. In any case, the amount of "Auto-

TF-ing" required for the elements attacking the Tripoli airport added to their problems and detracted from their success.

The problems referred to were well known early in the mission to the commanders aboard the lead KC-10 tanker. When the time had come to send home the spares, the lead pilot of the "Puffy" element had made tough decisions that Major General Forgan and Colonel Westbrook had accepted. The aircraft in "Puffy" and "Lujac" were suffering from a variety of ills even at that stage of the mission: one had just one functioning afterburner; others had lesser problems that could affect their weapons delivery capabilities. After sorting it all out, the best six jets of the eight in question proceeded with the attack. But one of the wing's most experienced crews had to go home in a malfunctioning Aardvark while some relatively inexperienced crews proceeded with the attack. This was another factor that affected the overall success of the bombing of the Tripoli airport.

One of the small complications of integrating this old plan with the attacks chosen against Azziziyah and Sidi Balal turned out to be use of the radio. The first mandatory radio call of the mission for the 48th's F-111Fs was the post-strike "Feet Wet" call. Explained in detail in the next chapter, this transmission was designed to alert the mission's command and control agencies, both Navy and Air Force, that each airplane had completed its attack and was northbound toward its tanker. It also gave a coded assessment by the crew of their attack's success or failure.

No one had anticipated that the "Feet Wet" calls of the earlier attackers would interfere with the bombing of the Tripoli airport. But Lieutenant Colonel F. and others found themselves distracted and perplexed by the recurring radio traffic from the fighter bombers ahead. After hours of almost total silence, the airwaves were suddenly full of radio chatter that coincided with the period of greatest activity and concentration in the "Puffy" and "Lujac" cockpits. The "Feet Wet" calls were bad; but the unexpected additional chatter from the Navy defense suppressors, in what seemed to be personal and unfathomable codes, was even worse. Finally, the series of several radio calls between a limping F-111, struggling with a failing electrical system, and the Navy agency tasked with giving each aircraft a heading vector to fly in order to find its tanker proved to be the worst of all. The pilots and WSOs of "Puffy" and "Lujac" tried to filter out all these nonessential audio inputs with varying degrees of success. Although minor, the problem was another complication which none of them needed—their mission was tough enough!

Nonessential visual inputs were another, even greater, problem. As this force closed on the airport, miles ahead a huge display of exploding bombs, blazing SAMs, and criss-crossing Triple-A tracers competed for their attention. Colonel Westbrook had realized that this impressive show would pose a real threat to the later attackers: if they were diverted from their critical cockpit duties, the results could be just as fatal as any direct hit. He had warned the crews during their final briefing that they would have to fight the temptation to stare at the incredible scene that would greet them. The WSO in "Puffy-11" momentarily forgot that advice as he raised his head from the radar scope for a few seconds to take in the memorable skyscape ahead. His pilot, Lieutenant Colonel F., brusquely reminded him to get back in the scope—he had work to do! Within minutes, Captain N. was able to return the favor. But first, this crew would deliver the bombs immortalized on videotape that would destroy or damage several Soviet-built "Candid" transport aircraft. Seen repeatedly on news telecasts all over the world, the crystal-clear video of their hard maneuvering to line up on the target aircraft and the subsequent fall and impact of their bombs would document the raid's concentration on military targets. Captain N. was surprised that the big transports were still there—he had assumed that the Libyans would disperse them as a defensive measure. After release of their twelve MK-82 AIRs, Lieutenant Colonel F. initiated a hard turn to the egress heading at low altitude. He then instinctively looked over his shoulder to see (and, out of habit, score) the bomb impacts. Captain N. quickly reminded him to watch the instruments, and especially his altitude!

The crew coordination displayed in the cockpit of "Puffy-11" was typical of what went on in most of the F-111Fs attacking Tripoli that night. Unfortunately, good crews cannot always compensate for problem aircraft. In more than one case, minor equipment malfunctions caused some of the eleven attackers that actually dropped their bombs to miss their targets. This proved true for at least two of the remaining fighter bombers assigned to the military side of the Tripoli airport. These equipment problems combined with human error reduced the success rate in the attack on the airport to only one completely successful F-111F out of six. The others had bombs impact near their respective aiming points, including military helicopters on the field and an operations building, but caused only minimal damage. The good news for the men flying those jets was that the Libyan defenses were not a big part of their problem. The defenses near the Tripoli airport reacted in a sporadic, ineffective manner, due to the tactical surprise achieved at this target.

The dusty old plan to strike the airport had been devised months earlier, but it still worked very well. Its success, though marred by the predictable difficulties of this marathon mission, affirmed the confidence the 48th TFW had always had in its ability to conduct a small, punishing raid on Libya with relative impunity. Unfortunately, that small raid was never ordered. Instead, with less than seventy-two hours to go before the TOTs, much to the surprise of all the participants, the mission's size had been tripled.

### APRIL 12–14, 1986

### COUNTDOWN TO COMBAT

On Saturday, April 12, the stage was set for the series of decisions that would cost the lives of two of the 48th Wing's finest crewmen. Faced with what appeared to be conflicting guidance on the Rules of Engagement, Major General McInerney and Colonel Westbrook flew to Ramstein, Germany, in an attempt to clarify the orders. What exactly was meant by inflicting "maximum visible damage" while assuring "minimum collateral damage"? Which of these somewhat incompatible goals had priority? Did we need to adjust our weapons loads in any way as a result?

General Donnelly met with McInerney and Westbrook that morning to discuss the situation. His guidance with respect to the ROE was clear and logical. First, no one anticipated that the mission could be conducted without causing some collateral damage. With that in mind, "maximum visible damage" was the primary goal—minimizing civilian casualties and damage to nonmilitary structures was a close second. Therefore, the planned bomb loads did not require any change.

During the course of this discussion, General Donnelly strayed from the subject of ROE, making a statement which got the attention of both of his subordinates. He mentioned that some airplanes might well be lost in the course of the mission. Major General McInerney asked if he really meant that; McInerney firmly believed that there was no target in Libya worth the loss of one of our crews and aircraft. The unstated assumption behind his question appears to have been that, if the loss of a jet was likely using the current plan, that plan should be changed.

General Donnelly answered by saying that the Air Force's job was to destroy its assigned targets—other considerations were secondary. That simple statement, and the inferences drawn by his listeners, would play a large part in the tactical error that would lead to the loss of "Karma-52."

At the time of the statement, the tactical error referred to had not yet been made. As McInerney and Westbrook flew back to Lakenheath Saturday afternoon, the final force composition against the three Air Force targets at Tripoli was still undecided. And, for a while it appeared that the wing would be given a chance to contribute to that decision.

That Saturday night, April 12, was the occasion for the 48th Wing's annual "Good Neighbor" awards banquet. This event was a much-anticipated community relations exercise, during which we honored many of our British friends from the surrounding Suffolk villages. Blessed with a local population which was decidedly pro-American, we had been looking forward to this party for some time. And, despite the imminent raid on Libya or perhaps because of it, there appeared to be no way that the event could be canceled.

Joyce and I had returned from London that Saturday after spending two nights there and attending a concert at Royal Albert Hall. The trip to London had been approved after Colonel Westbrook and I had reviewed a classified message on Wednesday. It had indicated that approval by Her Majesty's government of the use of F-111s based in Britain for a strike against Libya was very unlikely. Our assumption was that we would not take part in any raid unless Mrs. Thatcher gave her approval. Under the circumstances, Sam granted my request to go to London for a much needed break. (Later, he was just as surprised as the rest of us when the Iron Lady gave her strong "thumbs up" to the attack.) By the time I returned to Lakenheath early Saturday afternoon, the mission's execute orders were in hand.

As the party progressed that Saturday night, we found ourselves more than a bit constrained by our knowledge of the continuing countdown to the Monday afternoon takeoff. Our attempts to go on with business as usual were not entirely successful—the party was interrupted around ten o'clock when Lt. Col. Bob Pastusek, chief of the wing's offensive operations branch and, since January, a key planning officer for this contingency, brought us news.

The wing had been told earlier that day, for the first time, that eighteen planes would probably be used in the attack. For over three months, we had been planning for a small, surgical raid by no more than six jets. Now, however, with very little time left to adjust, the size of the mission had tripled—perhaps. If that was not enough to complicate the situation, the final word on whether the French would allow overflight did not arrive until late that evening. That unfortunate decision was negative for reasons even the French could not adequately explain afterward. It may be that Vernon Walters, the U.S. ambassador to the United Nations, talked to the wrong French government spokesman. Or perhaps it had something to do with the fact that a new French Minister of Defense had just taken office—some sources suggest that the new minister was unaware of a prior informal agreement made by his predecessor and was offended that he had not been consulted. Certainly, the French could not have already forgotten the recent terrorist attacks that had spilled blood in the streets of Paris. In any case, the information that Paris had responded with a firm *non* was accompanied by orders that the decision to use eighteen jets was definite.

After fifteen weeks of preparation, it was incredible to all of us that major changes to the targets, to the route of flight, and especially to the raid's size were all being made within forty-eight hours of the planned takeoff time. The impact on all aspects of the final planning was amazing. The biggest contributor was the

sheer number of aircrews brought into the planning process at
the last minute. As David Martin pointed out in the 1988 book
about combating terrorism, *Best Laid Plans*, at least the F-111
crews were on the scene. Many of the tanker crews were en route
to England without a clue as to what they would be asked to do
upon arrival.

Those new crews found a hornets' nest of activity at Lakenheath as everyone worked feverishly to make the mission work.
At times the atmosphere became heated. One such instance occurred when the tanker planners and fighter planners came to an
impasse over whether each cell of three F-111s could stay with
a single tanker from takeoff to drop-off—changing from tanker to
tanker at night without using radios would be an almost impossible task to coordinate at this late stage of the mission's planning.
The first tankers' answer was "impossible," but after further
study, a way was found. The tanker commander at RAF Mildenhall, an experienced colonel, took charge of the effort and led
his tanker operations staff to make changes that resulted in a simple "Mother Tanker" plan that worked well without communications. It was fortunate that a simple plan was finally devised:
many of the newly arrived tanker crews barely had time after
their arrival to grab a nap, refuel, and pick up their flight plans
for the actual mission. The remaining mission details were
known only to the fighters and to the command elements aboard
two lead tankers.

Other problems included F-111 crew selection; preparations
for a small raid had never required more than a dozen crews to
be involved at any one time. Now double that number would be
flying as primary and spare crews; several others would be needed
in critical ground support roles. Total crew availability was not
the problem—every man who knew about the mission wanted to
fly, and those who had been excluded from the process since
January were eager to get involved. The problem was selecting
the best twenty-four aircrews from such a long list. Colonel Westbrook put this decision in the hands of the squadron commanders
who flew with and observed their pilots and WSOs on a daily
basis. They applied their best judgement to the decision, and
produced an impressive final lineup. Nevertheless, some of those
added in the final seventy-two hours had not received any partic-

ular training in preparation for the raid. They also would have only a few hours to study their flight and attack plans. The latter would be further delayed because one last decision had still not been made: how many F-111Fs would attack each of the three targets?

The news that Lt. Col. Pastusek brought to the officers' club was considered to be a good omen. The wing had assumed that the distribution of eighteen planes would result in six jets for each of the three targets: Qaddafi's headquarters at the Azziziyah Barracks, the Sidi Balal terrorist training camp, and the military side of the Tripoli airport. Now, he reported that we had been asked how, if given our choice, we would redistribute those eighteen aircraft.

It was an intelligent question. The fact that it was being asked at all boded well for the success of the mission—despite the press of time, the men who would fly the raid were still being asked to make the key tactical decisions. Our crews had the most intimate knowledge of the targets, their defenses, and the problems that were likely to occur in striking them. The 48th's pilots and WSOs had been told what to strike, when to strike, and even some of the why. But they were the ones answering all of the "how" questions. Unlike other recent U.S. military debacles, this one was being done right.

Lieutenant Colonel Pastusek first took the question to Lieutenant Colonel F. who would be leading the mission. A quick review of the targets and their defenses led to the following recommendations. Only three jets should be sent against Sidi Balal: there was not enough of value in the target area to justify more. Nine jets should attack the Tripoli airport: it was relatively remote; it was lightly defended; and it was a high value target that guaranteed visible damage and helped ensure against collateral damage. Finally, and most importantly, no more than six jets should be used to attack Azziziyah Barracks.

This final recommendation was based on several obvious factors. Azziziyah was a relatively small target complex in the center of an urban area. For that reason, precision weapons—laser-guided, 2,000-pound GBU-10 bombs—would be utilized. For these weapons to guide correctly, the target must remain visible to both the bomb and the attacking aircraft. Sending six jets raised the possibility that aim points would be obscured by smoke and debris from preceding attackers even if the winds were exactly as forecast. Number six in line would have to find his target while looking through the chaos caused by twenty 2,000-pound bomb explosions. If laser guidance was lost, his weapons would fall ballistically, landing within the complex but unlikely to strike their intended pinpoint target.

The proximity to urban Tripoli also increased the odds that unintended collateral damage could occur. A mistake made in attacking Sidi Balal or Tripoli airport would be bad, but not as bloody as what might occur in downtown Tripoli. Sending more jets against Azziziyah would increase the chances that this might happen.

Finally, Azziziyah was the most heavily defended target. For reasons that I will later explain in detail, attacking this target with a large number of aircraft increased the odds that one or more of them would be damaged or shot down. Lieutenant Colonel F. felt strongly that six jets across Azziziyah was a maximum; even that number might produce casualties.

Lieutenant Colonel Pastusek carried Lieutenant Colonel F.'s recommendations to Colonel Westbrook at the officer's club. Sam and I slipped away from the main party room to hear the news. While we were still not pleased with the entire concept of a large raid, this information was very welcome. Nine jets against Tripoli airport made sense, as did three against Sidi Balal. Six attackers going to Azziziyah did not inspire supreme confidence, but it was within reason. Sam readily agreed with his staff's recommendations, and we rejoined the party feeling just a bit better about the raid and its chances for success.

The festivities wound down around midnight. I drove Joyce to our quarters, and then headed for the 494 TFS where route and target planning was still underway. Shortly after arriving there, I learned to my surprise that the 48th Wing's recommendations regarding airplanes-per-target had already been overruled. Worse, we were not back to six planes for each target; instead, we had been ordered to attack Azziziyah with nine F-111Fs, Tripoli airport with six, and Sidi Balal with three. A gross tactical error was being made, and it was being done against the best judgement of the people who were planning and flying the mission.

Nine airplanes attacking the most heavily defended target was too many. If not losing an airplane was still a major consideration, the decision to send that many jets over downtown Tripoli was clearly a mistake.

Why was the decision so obviously wrong? In order to understand, the reader must first know something about tactical bombing. One of the greatest dangers to an aircraft dropping bombs comes from its own weapons, or from those of other aircraft in the formation. There is always a possibility of being shot down by fragments from your own bombs or from your wingman's. In an attack involving multiple aircraft, a tactical planner is faced with the problem of ensuring separation from all bombs, using time or space, while minimizing the total time in the dangerous target area.

Extended time over the target means added exposure to the defenses: SAMs, Triple-A, and enemy fighters deployed to shoot you down if they can. If those defenses are able to concentrate on one aircraft at a time, their chances for shooting down jets go way up. For this reason, daytime bombing missions often use highly coordinated, simultaneous attacks from several points on the compass. This allows a large number of attacking jets to get on and off target in minimum time, overloading the defenses for the few seconds that the attackers are exposed. The hope is that this saturation effect will decrease aircraft losses—during my bombing missions over Southeast Asia, it was always comforting to think that the gunners were shooting at the other F-105s and not at mine. In daylight, the jets usually avoid each other's bombs by maintaining a specified minimum altitude higher than that of the highest predicted bomb fragments.

At night, this technique does not work, especially if the attackers are using low-level attack tactics. Why choose a night attack if it has such limitations? Because of its obvious benefits: it decreases the effectiveness of both enemy SAMs (some of which rely on optical and infrared guidance) and aimed Triple-A; and, depending on the opposing air force, it can almost totally remove the threat of interception. That was the case in Libya in 1986—the Libyan Air Force, while relatively large, was considered to have very little night fighting capability. The results of the raid confirmed that assessment.

But a night attack meant that the primary method for separating F-111s from each other and from bomb fragments was correct timing. The Pave Tack Toss maneuver would ensure adequate clearance from bomb fragments since it keeps the attacking aircraft well clear of the target area; fragments from a 2,000-pound bomb can travel as far as half a mile. But a minimum spacing of thirty seconds between jets was still needed for safety: the night attack dictated this as an adequate margin between the attacking aircraft. Thirty seconds translates into four-to-five nautical miles' spacing, which is considered comfortable in the dark. As a result, each additional airplane assigned to a target added another thirty seconds to the total time over that target, providing the defenses with additional reaction time and adding to the odds that the later jets would be damaged or shot down.

All of our planning in the months preceding the raid had been based on the premise that, next to the success of the mission as defined by bombs on target, preventing the loss of an airplane was the paramount consideration. This goal had been stressed in several of the directive messages from above the wing. For that reason, we had never recommended assigning more than six jets to a target so that the total time over target would not exceed two and a half minutes. Our concern had prompted us to recommend a maximum of six aircraft for another target in a message sent as far back as January 8.

Now, at the eleventh hour, we found ourselves ordered to send nine jets across the most difficult target we had considered. The last F-111F in line would not release its bombs until over four minutes after the leader! It was highly probable that one or more of the later aircraft would get hosed by the fully alerted defenses. Would we lose an aircraft and its crew? No one knew, but several of us were convinced that the risks had suddenly become much too high.

With only thirty-six hours to go to the mission's takeoff, whatever changes could be made would have to be made soon or not at all. We knew that the decision to overrule the wing's recommendation had come from a high level—Major General Forgan had communicated it to us, a strong indicator that it came from his boss, Gen. Charles Donnelly, the commander in chief of U.S. Air Forces in Europe, or higher. I guessed that it had come from above Donnelly—from the deputy commander in chief of EUCOM (the European Command encompassing all U.S. forces in Europe) at Stuttgart, Air Force Gen. Richard Lawson. General Lawson and his boss, Army Gen. Bernard Rogers, had been criticized for their involvement, or lack of same, in the decisions that led to the deaths of over 200 marines in Lebanon in 1983, and for the subsequent botched Navy airstrike against terrorist targets in Lebanon. The tactical error that sent the Navy jets over Lebanon at sunrise rather than at night or at high noon may have been made in Washington, but it was put into operation by EUCOM at Stuttgart. Although an experienced strategic bomber pilot, General Lawson's knowledge of fighters and their tactics was not all-encompassing.

It seemed logical to assume that EUCOM might be the source of our 1986 tactical error as well—General Donnelly knew too much about fighters and tactics. If that was right, then convincing Major General McInerney ought to be the key to getting the plan changed. He would then approach General Donnelly, who in turn would strongly suggest the change to General Lawson. Faced with the professional judgement of two highly experienced fighter generals, Lawson would change the plan. That was the scenario I envisioned as the final briefing to Major General McInerney approached. If he agreed and acted quickly, we could still have over twenty-four hours to accomplish the necessary changes. I anticipated that sequence of events without knowledge of the preceding day's conversation between Generals Donnelly and McInerney and Colonel Westbrook.

At this point, a reminder about post-mission claims regarding responsibility for the decision is appropriate. As reported in *Best Laid Plans* and confirmed in correspondence, General Donnelly has always assumed full responsibility for the allocation of the Tripoli strike forces. If his recollections are correct, my assumptions about getting General Lawson to change his mind were mistaken. But General Donnelly further states that he followed the recommendations of 48th Wing planners in deciding on the distribution of the attackers. My research on this subject, including interviews with several of those directly involved both at Lakenheath and Ramstein, reveals no evidence to support that statement. In fact, two conversations that night between Lieutenant Colonel Pastusek and Major General Forgan strongly suggest that no one in the wing ever made such a recommendation.

When Bob Pastusek left the officers' club with Colonel Westbrook's instructions, he immediately returned to the 494 TFS and telephoned HQ USAFE to make the wing's preferred distribution of aircraft per target known. He ended up speaking directly to Major General Forgan, a trusted superior for whom he had worked in previous assignments. Forgan seemed to accept the wing's recommendations without reservation, and Lieutenant Colonel Pastusek recalls that when the conversation ended he was left with the impression that there would be no further changes.

But hours later, at about the time I was discovering that a change had been ordered, Lieutenant Colonel Pastusek and Major General Forgan were again talking on a secure phone line. Bob had not taken the call that ordered the change, so he too was surprised and disturbed when he found out about it. Despite the hour (it was now almost 1 A.M. on April 13), he called HQ USAFE again and was able to reach Major General Forgan once more. Lieutenant Colonel Pastusek communicated his strong disagreement with the change that had been made, indicating that the 48th believed it was a "high-risk, low-payoff" gamble. He recalls being cut short by the general's abrupt reply that the decision had been made above USAFE, at EUCOM, and that we now had our orders. Bob hung up the phone having separately reached the same conclusion as I: the evidence indicated that General Lawson or his staff had made the change. Of course, General Donnelly's post-mission assumption of responsibility for the decision contradicts this conclusion.

At the time these events were occurring, I believed that the final briefing to Major General McInerney provided the best and perhaps the only opportunity to get the decision changed. The briefing to the general convened in the main briefing room of the 494th on Sunday afternoon, April 13. The audience was small: my recollection is that those present were Major General McInerney, his command's deputy for operations Col. Steve Ridgway, Sam Westbrook, Tom Yax, Ed Dunivant, our four flying squadron commanders, and myself. The primary briefer was the squadron commander who would be leading the force, Lieutenant Colonel F. As we began, I was struck by the irony of the situation: after three and a half months of trying to keep the Third Air Force commander up to date and in the loop, we were now briefing him on a plan he had never seen before—a plan we would be executing within thirty-six hours. It was obvious to all concerned that much of what he would be hearing was, from his perspective, a fait accompli. The only substantive question was whether the potentially fatal tactical error could be reversed.

The briefing generated little comment until that element of the plan came up. At that point, Major General McInerney seized on the error without hesitation, noting that nine jets across downtown Tripoli was too many and that we would certainly be criticized if we lost an aircraft under the circumstances. His comments were delivered with some emphasis, but without interrupting the flow of the briefing—this first opportunity to argue for a change was lost when none of us made a specific comment to reinforce his visible concern with the plan. Instead, the briefing continued with the gravity of the error seeming to fade under the weight of the plan's intricate details. Getting the large force to and from its targets on this longest fighter mission ever took up a lot of briefing time—at least thirty minutes had passed before another opportunity developed to drive home the need for a change. I could not let this second, and perhaps final, chance pass.

A key point that the general seemed to have missed was who had made the decision to send nine F-111Fs to the most heavily defended target. The general's earlier critical comments appeared to have been directed to those of us in the room. We had not immediately corrected the impression that the error was ours. As the briefing concluded, Major General McInerney gave us an opening: he asked if there was anything, anything at all, he could do to help ensure the success of the mission. Several seconds of silence ensued.

Blissfully unaware of the impact of General Donnelly's Saturday comment that aircraft might well be lost, I thought this was a critical moment. I did not know why Sam Westbrook had not chimed in—perhaps I had interrupted him before he could start, or maybe he was waiting for a private moment with the general to make his argument. In any case, I waited as long as I could before breaking the silence. With the floor now mine, I tried to make the point as quickly and persuasively as possible.

The general had correctly identified the plan's Achilles heel, I said. What he might not know was that the wing shared his misgivings and had, in fact, recommended a different distribution of F-111Fs per target. We had been overruled. We did not know who had made the decision, but we considered it a serious error that could cost us men and airplanes. What could he do to help ensure the mission's success? He could get that decision changed. What specific change would we suggest? A return to the numbers per target that the wing had recommended on Saturday night would be one option. If there was not enough time for that, a reduction in the size of the attack from eighteen to fifteen aircraft would also work—simply scrub the last three F-111Fs slated for Azziziyah and all their support forces.

Major General McInerney listened attentively, but his mind was already made up. So was Colonel Westbrook's. They had heard Donnelly's comments the day before, and they understood that either he or someone above him in the chain of command had made this tactical decision. Striking the targets was primary; all other considerations were secondary. As a result, they would make no attempt to reverse the decision. It was obvious that they both shared our concerns about losing men and jets. It was also clear to them and to everyone in the room that Sunday that a mistake was being made that could cost American lives. But, to those who had heard them, General Donnelly's earlier words seemed to preclude any further discussion or dissent.

My hope for a strong supporting vote from the general faded immediately. With his decision made, he shifted the discussion from correcting the mistake to somehow limiting its negative impact. Perhaps, he suggested, we could come up with some innovative tactical measures to solve the problem. He asked what changes could be made to lessen the danger to the last three aircraft. Could they toss their bombs a greater distance in order to stay further away from the defenses? The fact was that our F-111s were attacking at nearly the maximum speed allowed for their weapons loads—no appreciable improvement in standoff was possible.

That was the extent of the solutions offered; we all understood that there were no other workable options if the plan could not be changed. Our crews would have to fend for themselves. Despite our recognition that a tactical blunder was taking place, there was no concerted effort to change the plan after the final briefing to Major General McInerney. Neither Sam Westbrook nor I attempted to raise the issue over the general's head. A telephone conversation may have taken place between McInerney and Forgan, but such a peer discussion would have been unlikely to elevate our concern to a level where the decision might have been reversed.

Instead, at the briefing's conclusion, McInerney huddled with Westbrook and suggested that the last crews slated for Azziziyah be told to watch the situation closely; if the defenses seemed too tough, they should be prepared to break off their attacks rather than risk being shot down. This was passed on to Lieutenant Colonel F. and eventually to the six men involved. Unfortunately, the only option they were given was an untenable one. It is utterly against both the training and the instinct of fighter crewmen to abort a mission because they might be hurt. While none of the last three in line against Azziziyah succeeded in striking their targets, preemptive aborts did not occur. The crew of "Karma-51" dropped the bombs that resulted in the heavy civilian casualties near the French embassy. "Karma-53" aborted due to an aircraft malfunction prior to releasing weapons. And "Karma-52" was shot down before it completed its attack.

My raising the issue had not had the impact I had hoped for—the plan would not be changed. Frustrated, I volunteered to lead that last three-ship element across Tripoli, using the rationale that the presence of a grizzled combat veteran would give our young aviators added confidence. In the position they would be flying, they would need all the confidence they could get. My request was denied; in the end, none of the wing's colonels flew on the mission.

The explanation is simple. Colonel Westbrook made the decisions as to what each of our roles would be. My 150 hours of F-111 time were probably considered inadequate, and someone had to command the wing at Lakenheath during the fourteen-hour mission. Colonel Yax was fighting a very bad cold and could not fly despite his high proficiency—Colonel Westbrook had decided against Tom's participation after noting his physical condition while flying to Germany on Saturday, April 12. He was assigned to the control tower to coordinate the mission's launch. Col. Ed Dunivant, our assistant deputy commander for operations and also a volunteer, was assigned to a command and control position in one of the KC-10s. And Colonel Westbrook decided to take a command position on the lead KC-10 tanker with Major General Forgan.

This last decision has been the subject of discussion and conjecture since the raid; Sam Westbrook has admitted that he is often asked why he did not lead the mission. The fact is that Sam Westbrook made the very logical decision that the raid's success was too important to risk. One of the wing's squadron commanders, who had been concentrating on leading a small raid and who had been receiving extra training for over three months, would be more likely to achieve that success. Sam made a decision with his head that many of us, including the author, might have made with our gut. It is fair to say that some number of those who would have made the emotional decision to be out front would have also made inadvertent errors that could have jeopardized the mission. Col. Sam W. Westbrook III held his ego in check and made the right call; the chances for the success of Operation El Dorado Canyon were significantly enhanced as a result.

While he apparently did not ask for a change to the plan, Major General McInerney was still very much concerned with the welfare of the crews in those last three jets over downtown Tripoli. This became evident a few hours later during his final comments to all the selected El Dorado Canyon aircrews. In those remarks, delivered in the packed, hushed main briefing room of the 494th, he identified some of the crewmen of the "Karma" element by name, and encouraged them to watch themselves because of the tough position they would be in. Finally, he asked if they had any problems with or comments about the mission as modified. With that remark providing the only evidence that a problem had been recognized, the matter of the three extra jets was put to bed for good. For obvious reasons, there are some who might hope that it would never be raised again. The surviving four crewmen of the "Karma" element are not among them.

In the final hours prior to takeoff, they digested the facts, assessed their situation, and came to their own conclusions about their chances for survival.

In hindsight, it appears obvious that the decision should have been changed. As documented in *Best Laid Plans*, General Donnelly's rationale for the decision he claims—to increase the Probability of Damage, PD—is not convincing in the author's judgement. PD against any particular aim point only increases if the number of aircraft attacking that aim point goes up. Five of the seven aim points at Azziziyah were to be attacked by single aircraft; no cumulative increase in PD occurred for them. The other two aim points had two jets assigned to each; if they merited that much firepower, four of a reduced force of only six attackers could have struck them just as well. It is noteworthy that some senior F-111 pilots and WSOs believe that an individual, well-defended target merits at least three attackers if the desired PD is over seventy-five percent, but the El Dorado Canyon force, despite its size, was too small to be used in that manner. Their rationale is based on experience with all the multiple problems that can occur when trying to deliver precision munitions.

Why were the grave concerns with the decision not brought to General Donnelly's attention? This question may be problematical: no one knows whether he would have made a change or recommended a change even if he had been aware of our misgivings. The fact remains that the dissent from the trenches never reached the decision maker. It was our responsibility to point out the error in the hope that it might be corrected. We failed in that responsibility.

Faced with a late afternoon takeoff on April 14 and the prospect of the longest fighter mission they would ever be ordered to fly, the crews had a limited amount of time to complete their planning, gather their thoughts, and get some much needed rest before starting the marathon. After the mass briefings were completed that Sunday night, the crews remained in the 494th to complete the final details of their planning. Most would remain awake into the early hours of Monday morning, trying to put the finishing touches on their knowledge of the routes, targets, weapons, etc., while getting tired enough to ensure sleep despite their pre-mission jitters. Those nerves were understandable considering the circumstances. Over ninety percent of them were about to fly their first combat mission. For most, it would be the longest sortie they had ever flown in a fighter—a few may have flown longer, boring transoceanic deployments in other aircraft. Over Libya, they would encounter the most technically sophisticated defenses any air force had thus far faced. And the mission would be flown at night, when all the challenges and hazards of fighter aviation are increased. Finally, some of them had been forewarned that their positions in the attacking formation would be especially hazardous. It is not surprising that most of the men thought seriously about life—and death.

Some of the men took the time needed to check and update their wills. Others were also concerned about their spiritual well-being. At least one of the men, a devout Roman Catholic, sought out a Catholic chaplain and took part in the sacraments of Penance and Communion. Once sufficiently exhausted, the crews slept. Rooms on base were made available at the visiting officers' quarters but few, if any, chose this option. Most of the 48th's pilots and WSOs slept in their own beds that night, trying not to betray their excitement and apprehension. All had the option of taking a sleeping pill to overcome their nerves, and several did. Despite the chemical assistance, a number of them would get little quality sleep that Sunday night—their minds were too filled with the myriad details they had to know to survive the next night. And, unfortunately, some were still worried about how and when they would get those details.

There was still some continuing turmoil due to the last-minute, three-fold expansion of the raid. In the case of Qaddafi's headquarters, the large number of attacking aircraft made selection of desired bomb impact points, DMPIs (pronounced "dim-pies" for Desired Mean Point of Impact), very critical. Surface winds at the time of the attack would dictate which targets in the complex would have to be attacked first. If the wrong sequence was chosen, the later aircraft in the stream would have their targets obscured by smoke from the earlier bombs. This meant that the selection of aiming points for each attacker, completed on Sunday, could well have been changed up until just a few hours before takeoff. At that time, if the best estimate of predicted surface winds at Tripoli had changed, the final selection of DMPIs would have also been modified. Luckily, this proved unnecessary. Unluckily, the predicted winds proved to be far off the mark.

My own rest that Sunday night was confined to a brief, fitful sleep before reporting to the command post early Monday morning. The normal twelve-hour exercise shift was not going to be a factor on April 14—I settled in for what would be at least a twenty-four-hour grind.

Adrenaline would help, but first its effects had to be hidden as we attempted to conduct what we hoped would appear to the outside world, and to many of our own people, to be a normal peacetime exercise. F-111s were being flown on training missions at a very low sortie rate, but the decreased pace of activity was not severe enough to betray our large-scale preparations for the attack. Other normal exercise activities were also going on, but with some unusual restrictions. Fighters from other wings were normally scheduled to simulate "attacks" on our base, but none appeared that day—the distractions associated with such attacks could be dangerous while dealing with live ordnance! The "attacks" were also normally punctuated by explosions of smoke and concussion grenades to add realism to the exercise. None were used that Monday—too many of the wing's security forces knew that something big was happening and their nerves did not need additional stress.

By two o'clock that afternoon, the crews had begun arriving at the 494th's building. Those slated to bring up the rear of the long line attacking Colonel Qaddafi's headquarters checked quickly to see if the plan had been modified. They showed no outward signs of disappointment when they found that it had not been changed.

Elsewhere around the base, various incidents took place as the unusual aspects of our "exercise" caused people of all ranks to question what was going on. Some, despite their rank and experience, had no idea; others, in spite of their relative inexperience, had long since reached the right conclusions. That afternoon, a senior NCO stood in line at the base's Quick Shop, a military 7-Eleven-style convenience store, wondering aloud why the entire quarterly allotment of live bomb fuses was being used up in this exercise.[5] Listeners who knew what was happening cringed, but held their tongues rather than lend emphasis to his security violation. A few hours later, a young airman was overheard talking to friends or family on a pay phone in the NCO club. Feeling no pain after more than a few beers, he loudly told the stateside listener that the 48th was just about ready to "Bomb the hell out of Qaddafi." Security police responded to the club to silence this indiscreet caller, but he was never found or identified.[6]

In the midst of this controlled chaos, Colonel Westbrook prepared to depart for Mildenhall to board the lead KC-10 with Major General Forgan. Sam's day had been spent escorting the Air Force chief of staff, General Gabriel, around the base so that he could view our "exercise." Surprisingly, both the exercise and General Gabriel's visit had been on our schedule months before we were even alerted for a possible airstrike against Libya. While it was purely coincidental that the raid was ordered on that date, it is also very likely that we would have generated a no-notice exercise if one had not been scheduled. Perhaps General Gabriel would have gone out of his way to be there as well. In any case, when Sam and I solemnly shook hands, wishing each other good luck as he left Lakenheath, I found myself wondering how many men and planes would be lost. That losses would occur seemed a given.

While the planes were en route to their targets, we took action at Lakenheath to deal with that eventuality. Chaplains, personal affairs specialists, and a few doctors were ordered to stay close to their phones in case they were needed. The Air Force, like each of the military services, has a well-practiced routine for dealing with casualties both in peace- and in wartime. Unfortunately, in the real world, the sad process is never routine. We were about to find that out again as midnight, Greenwich mean time, approached.

Gen. Charles Gabriel, Maj. Gen. Thomas G. McInerney, and Lt. Gen. John Shaud, a member of the chief's staff, had returned to Lakenheath after 11 P.M. in order to be on the scene when the attack took place. The nine stars in the command post were no big surprise to our people after the mid-afternoon announcement that the wing was conducting a top secret contingency combat operation. Up to that point, the command post had been run the way it would have been in a normal exercise: even the call signs and schedules for the actual mission had been kept hidden from the majority of personnel who had no need to know. With less than two hours remaining to takeoff, the wraps had come off the raid as we announced our combat footing after asking our British contingent to leave. The Royal Air Force Rapier missile unit assigned to help defend us against air attack filed out politely, but only after their commander volunteered that we should, "Hit the bastard hard!" Perhaps the presence at Mildenhall of what appeared to be every existing KC-10 in the USAF inventory had been the tip-off. Or, like the rest of us, he may have been watching or listening to the BBC—in the days preceding the raid, their reports had been uncomfortably accurate in predicting the upcoming mission. On the night of the actual raid, British media reports appeared to have been censored, perhaps in accordance with the Official Secrets Act; for the first time in weeks, they missed the mark by a wide margin.

But by then it was too late. The vague news reports broadcast on April 14 that "routine exercises" at both Lakenheath and Upper Heyford were being conducted under a tight veil of secrecy did not fool the British public. They certainly did not fool the waiting Libyans. Within minutes of the first bomb impacts, we found out that one of our planes was missing.

### CHAPTER SEVEN

# HEADING HOME

E very air combat mission has a distinct break point in its execution. Prior to that point, every action of the aircrew is devoted to the use of the aircraft and its weapons against the enemy. Missiles must be delivered, cannons must be fired, bombs must be dropped—all with the goal of doing as much damage to the target as possible. The plane is the transport vehicle for those weapons, and the crew is just the most complex "sensor system" used in employing both the plane and its weapons. During this period, it is said that the crew is working for Uncle Sam.

But all that changes in an instant. One reason for the change can be that the plane reaches a critical fuel state before all its weapons are expended, requiring the crew to cut short their attack in order to reach some friendly base. Another is that all weapons have been fired, a condition described by fighter pilots with the term "Winchester." That distinct radio call indicates a plane in which all offensive thinking, short of suicidal Kamikaze-style action, has ceased. At that moment, the crew begins working for themselves.

Most of the El Dorado Canyon F-111F crews reached this point the instant their bombs exploded on Libyan soil. Suddenly the pilots and WSOs shifted mental gears, realizing that the only real purpose for the rest of the mission was to get themselves and their jets safely home, or down as the case might be. The high-tech Aardvarks were no longer deadly; instead they were now merely expensive transportation systems needed to carry the crews back to England and Lakenheath.

But bomb impact was not a time to start celebrating and thinking about tomorrow. Relaxation and thoughts of families in East Anglia would have to wait until the Libyan defenses had been safely cleared. That process would require more than just leaving the Libyan SAM rings—circles on each aviator's map describing the maximum effective range expected from a given site. The possibility of a reaction to the raid by the Libyan Air Force was still quite real. No one in the attacking force could be sure that the Libyan pilots and planes would not get into the air that night. There was always a chance that the dozens of Syrian pilots known to be serving in Libya would turn out to be more proficient in night flying than their Libyan hosts. And even if the Libyan SAMs, Triple-A, and MiGs could be safely avoided, there remained the problem of successfully transiting the fully alerted defenses of the U.S. Sixth Fleet.

As pointed out earlier, the problem of potential fratricide had always been one of the 48th Wing's chief concerns. Fortunately, the Navy's "delousing" procedures proved to be simple and workable. Each northbound crew began the process with their first mandatory radio call of the mission, a brief "Feet Wet" call to the airborne command and control elements, both Air Force and Navy, which included a coded phrase to describe their success or failure. "Tranquil Tiger" indicated success, while "Frosty Freezer" marked an unsuccessful attack. The reader should note that computers pick these word combinations; certainly no one in the 48th would take credit for these tongue twisters. The only point of pride involved in the codes was the number of "Frosty Freezer" calls compared to the number of "Tranquil Tigers"; we all hoped that the ratio of successful attacks to aborts would be very high.

With the "Feet Wet" call having been completed at the appropriate point, Lieutenant Colonel F. concentrated on speed and altitude control as his jet sped northward in the darkness over the Mediterranean. Captain N. in the right seat focused on navigating to an exact point beyond which "Remit-31" would be free to go to its tanker. By adhering to a preplanned flight path, including certain altitude and airspeed restrictions, "Remit-31" was positively identifying itself as friendly to the understandably nervous Navy. Retaliatory attacks against the carriers would remain possible for many hours after the raid, and the fleet's defenses would remain at heightened alert states to defend against that event. But the biggest concern was that the Libyan Air Force would mix with the departing F-111s and A-6s in the raid's immediate aftermath. The "delousing" ballet would ensure that any such attempt would be discovered and intercepted—the F-14 Tomcats in nearby orbits were more than eager to add to the kill totals achieved in air battles with Libya as far back as 1981.

As each F-111 reached the end point of the "delousing" circuit, the temptation to relax grew stronger but was quickly suppressed by two realities. For those who had witnessed it, one of those realities was the memory of a huge fireball. Every survivor was asking himself the same question: whose plane had been shot down? No one yet knew who was missing. The final tally of call signs heard in the obligatory "Feet Wet" calls should have revealed which jet had been lost. But in the heat of battle, several circumstances combined to cause confusion. First, the aircraft that had aborted immediately after leaving its tanker had returned to the tanker without the need to make a post-strike radio call. In addition, one jet that had suffered a major electrical failure prior to the target had eventually found and joined on a tanker that was slated to receive only EF-111 aircraft. Finally, one crew flying an aircraft that was originally a spare may have inadvertently reverted to their previous call sign. The resulting confusion, based on some combination of these factors, made it seem as if at least two aircraft were missing. The problem would not be sorted out until several minutes after all the 48th's surviving planes had rejoined with their tankers for the trip home.

Those tankers were the other reality that prevented any premature relaxation—somewhere ahead in the blackness, they had to be found and joined with as soon as possible. The mission's briefing had been meticulous and detailed in most respects, but some crewmen recall that the post-strike tanker rendezvous received very little attention. As one pilot remembers, "There was little said beyond 'get a vector, head north, find your tanker, join on him, and get gas.'" While planning had assured that every plane would have sufficient fuel to recover to some friendly base if rendezvous with a tanker was missed, none of the pilots or WSOs were looking forward to the possibility of a night low-fuel landing at an unfamiliar base. Each and every crewman was intent on getting home to the friendly confines of RAF Lakenheath and to their waiting friends and families—the realization that at least two of their fellow airmen had been lost somehow added to the urgency to get back.

Initially, each crew received a vector—a suggested heading to fly to find their tanker—from the mission's command and control elements. These headings proved generally inaccurate—several crews recall only a generic 360-degree heading recommendation no matter where they were—resulting in some waste of precious fuel. Luckily, most F-111 crews also received early reassurance from their air-to-air Tactical Air Navigation (TACAN) systems. This system provides both direction and distance to a particular tanker identified by a preset frequency on its TACAN radio. But for those whose TACANs did not work immediately, the level of tension in the Aardvark cockpits rose dramatically.

Many of the crewmen shared the feeling of Major S. that the hunt for the tankers was "almost more nerve-wracking than the actual attack." Still alone in the dark, each Aardvark looked forward to seeing friendly faces again; especially faces with fuel to dispense. Despite painstaking planning, most of the 48th TFW's F-111Fs were now below their expected fuel states—a lot more afterburner had been used during the high-speed attacks than anticipated. To complicate the situation further, the tanker orbit points near Sicily were in the middle of several layers of high cirrus clouds. Low on fuel, following erroneous vectors, and discovering that their tankers could not be seen in the clouds, the pilots and WSOs tensed further as they searched the skies, first with their radars and then with their eyes, for the waiting airborne service stations.

Several rendezvous attempts resulted in near head-on passes and wrenching, fuel-wasting maneuvers to finish the process. Each Captain J. experienced this problem, one of them more than once. Each missed rendezvous added to the pressure on the

F-111 crews as already low fuel quantities were further depleted. At least one crew reached a state where it was very unlikely that they could safely divert to the nearest friendly base in Italy; they did not have enough gas remaining to get there. Their only choice was to either get on the tanker successfully or to eventually eject from their fuel-starved Aardvark. The crews who had already taken on some fuel and were now flying in formation with the tankers recognized the growing panic in the voices of their nearby buddies. As documented in *Best Laid Plans,* one savvy crew did what they could to help by dumping fuel and then lighting their afterburners. The resultant "torching" phenomenon was bright enough to be seen for many miles, and it did the job for the sweating F-111 crew nearby. Well below their preplanned bingo, they quickly found and joined with the tanker and finally began receiving fuel.

Once on the tanker, every crewman in every F-111 breathed a huge sigh of relief as the fuel transfer process began. Seeing your fuel quantity begin to increase after watching it inexorably decrease is an especially good feeling, guaranteed to soothe frazzled nerves in any cockpit. But no one could relax completely until every attacker was back on a tanker. Eventually, all of the surviving airplanes were safely rejoined with their tankers, although not necessarily with the particular tanker that had been expecting them. Once in tow, they took on fuel for the return trip to England while the sad, confused head count continued. The tanker element awaiting "Karma-52" orbited in its preplanned position while a communications search for the jet continued. The forlorn radio calls on the standard emergency "Guard" frequencies asking 52 to check in went unanswered. But there was still a chance that the plane was just damaged, unable to communicate, and would soon be landing at a friendly emergency recovery base. Eventually, with the previously mentioned call sign confusion sorted out, it became clear that just one plane was missing. As time passed, it also became certain that the missing plane had not miraculously turned up at one of the recovery fields.

In some F-111F cockpits, this somber delay was especially confusing and difficult. Some crews did not have complete lineup cards, so they were unsure which of their friends matched up with particular call signs. As it became clear that one aircraft had been lost, these crewmen listened closely to the repeated roll calls, trying to recognize voices in order to determine who was missing. Eventually they realized which crew had not returned, and their thoughts turned to their friends' present plight. The hope was that Captains Ribas-Dominicci and Lorence had successfully ejected and were floating in their capsule off the coast of Libya. That hope was tempered by the realization that the explosion they had witnessed, either on or above the water, might not have been survivable. In "Jewel-63"'s cockpit, the impact of the probable death of his friends and of the entire mission to that point was finally taking a toll on Captain J. After a tense, aborted rendezvous with the tanker and a hurried initial refueling, he felt the tension drain from him and be replaced by a reaction approaching shock. As he flew on the tanker's wing, thinking of Fernando and Paul, he suddenly felt physically ill. Struggling to keep from vomiting, he returned to the tanker's boom when his turn arrived, and discovered that he could not fly smoothly enough to again achieve a hookup. Eventually he overcame his queasiness and was successful in his subsequent refuelings, but it took nearly an hour before he felt close to normal.

For Major S. and Captain W. in "Karma-51," the reason they had never heard their wingman's "Feet Wet" call was clear at last: the radio call had never been made. "Karma-51" radioed to the lead tanker, "I don't think 'Karma-52' made it." With that added input, Major General Forgan reluctantly made the decision to head for home. By one hour after the attack, "Karma-52" and its crew were informally, but officially, declared missing in action. Prior to the mission, the fear of many in Washington had been that captured American airmen might be marched in chains through the streets of Tripoli. By 1:30 A.M. on April 15, that fear had become one of our best hopes in the Lakenheath command post. We anxiously awaited any additional information on the fate of Fernando Ribas-Dominicci and Paul Lorence.

Meanwhile, in the cockpits of the homeward-bound F-111s, widely varied post-adrenaline reactions were setting in. Feelings of physical discomfort were one response; Captain J.'s symptoms noted earlier were not unique. One sinking WSO took his "go" pill immediately after the first refueling; and then proceeded to

eat, drink, and mostly talk his way all the way back to Lakenheath—much to the annoyance of his silence-seeking pilot. Still,
the withdrawn pilot, avoiding his amphetamine and the dicey
side effects he remembered, finally gave in to his WSO's entreat-
ies to eat something. He then felt much better for the remainder
of the long, boring trip home.

That boredom was not shared in every Aardvark, however.
Various minor mechanical and electrical problems kept the trip
interesting for several crews. But the pilot and WSO of "Elton-
43" would have given anything to have only a minor problem.
Their abort in the target area had been caused by a "Wheelwell
Hot" indication that had totally disrupted their attack at nearly
the last moment. The light warns that a duct in the area of the
main landing gear is leaking hot engine air—a condition that
calls for quick action to prevent an inflight fire and possible loss
of the aircraft. This critical emergency recurred as they flew west,
and the crew struggled with the ticklish decision of what to do
and where to go. Eventually the emergency, with advice from
the mission's command elements, would dictate their course of
action. They would land safely at Rota airbase in Spain, the only
F-111F other than "Karma-52" that would not complete the long
round trip.

For those crews not struggling with a critical emergency, the
hours of night formation flying and refueling provided some of
the last remaining challenges of the mission. Their pre-combat
nervousness had disappeared, but everyone remained aware that
a moment's inattention could result in bent wingtips or worse.
My second trailer mate in Thailand was a survivor of a midair
collision during refueling operations—doctors at Fitzsimmon's
Army Hospital in Denver had done wonders with his facial
burns. The nagging concern remained that a mistake made by
an exhausted pilot would result in a similar, catastrophic midair
collision. All of us tried to push the images of burning wreckage,
spinning lazily to earth, out of our minds. Thanks to the skill of
the crewmen involved, those images did not become a reality.

The mission's world-record duration had its greatest effect on
each pilot and WSO during the seemingly endless trip home. I
cannot supply a detailed description of what it is like to spend
fourteen hours in a fighter cockpit—both because I have never

done it myself and because it is so far removed from the day-to-day experience of the average reader. The physiological and psychological effects are tremendous: the word "discomfort" is accurate but only if modified by terms like "cubed" or "to the Nth power." My own experience on a nine-hour combat mission suggests that, during the periods when cockpit activity is reduced, a huge amount of mental energy is needed just to ignore how miserable you are.

Perhaps a brief attempt should be made to describe the mission's length in layman's terms. If the comparison makes sense, it may help the reader imagine just how stressing Operation El Dorado Canyon was to its Air Force fighter participants. Imagine that you are on a round-trip night drive from your home to a destination six hours distant; Chicago to St. Louis is one such journey that comes to mind. Your car is a small sports model; something like a Porsche or a Corvette. You must wear a tight-fitting jump suit and a three-pound helmet the entire time. To complete the trip in minimum time, fuel is pumped by hose from an accompanying tanker truck. Once in the car and on the road, there is no stopping—refueling must be done on the go at normal cruise speeds (excellent "formation driving" skills are required; tailgating for several hours is a necessity). After six hours and nearing your destination, you must leave your friendly tanker and accelerate to near-maximum speed for a brief period during which the residents of your destination attempt to destroy you and your vehicle with all the firepower at their command. After that brief hair-raising experience, you must find your fuel truck in the dark again, and retrace the entire six-hour journey back to the starting point.

Of course, the entire trip is done with the top up and the windows closed—no standing or turning around—and without access to any roadside facilities. Like your Air Force counterparts, you may carry one or two "piddle packs," plastic containers that are difficult to use when standing and nearly impossible to use accurately when sitting down. You finally reach home again a full fourteen hours after starting your journey; only then can you open the car door and leave the tight confines of its cockpit.

All of this may still be difficult to imagine, but the hope remains that it conveys the spectrum of feelings—from hunger to

thirst, to bladder distress, to imminent claustrophobia—that be-
siege an individual under these conditions. While the reader may
still be puzzling over this problem, he or she may better understand the old Air Force saying that seems apropos in this situation: "I'd rather have a sharp stick in the eye!"

Fortunately, in the remaining hours of the return trip some
things happened that diverted the crews from their discomfort.
The most unusual of these occurred when someone broke the
general silence on the UHF radio frequency to suggest that everyone tune in to a particular high frequency (HF) broadcast. Those
who could receive it heard U.S. Armed Forces Radio in Europe
carrying a live feed of the White House press conference explaining the raid. Several pilots and WSOs who listened in, especially the Southeast Asia combat veterans, found it "eerie" to
hear Secretary of State George Shultz and Secretary of Defense
Caspar Weinberger giving details of a bombing mission that was
still in progress. With over four hours to go to Lakenheath, the
aircrews listened in rapt attention, some of them realizing for the
first time that they had just played a starring role in a story of
worldwide significance. The broadcast concluded with the Armed
Forces announcer dedicating his next two songs to those who had
just been in combat for their nation. Homeward bound, the
48th's El Dorado Canyon pilots and WSOs listened misty-eyed
as their helmets' earphones filled with "Anchors Aweigh" and the
"Air Force Song." One line from the latter predicts only two
likely fates for combat crewmen: "we live in fame or go down in
flame." They felt fortunate to have avoided the latter—two of
their buddies had not been so lucky. As to fame, they had no
idea that it would remain well beyond their reach. The anti-
terrorism nature of the record-breaking combat mission they were
completing would force them to remain anonymous for the foreseeable future.

One ironic aspect of the Washington news conference was the
reaction of the F-111 crews when they heard Secretary Weinberger being asked if it was true that the French embassy had
been bombed. Weinberger's immediate, surprised reaction was
that that was impossible. All of the listening pilots and WSOs,
including the crew that had dropped the stray bombs in question,
agreed with him, believing that the incident must have been in-

vented by the media or the Libyans. Within hours of landing, however, the truth of the charge would be known. El Dorado Canyon would prove once again that precision bombing is often imprecise—the realities of combat make it possible to limit, but never totally eliminate, unintended civilian casualties. The Desert Storm bombing campaign of 1991 has reinforced that lesson.

As the task force headed north after passing Gibraltar, "Elton-43"'s situation was finally judged to be serious enough to require a landing well short of the British Isles—the ailing jet would have to recover into the NATO airbase at Rota, Spain. "Elton-41" was initially told to escort "Elton-43" into Rota and land there as well, but its crew "won" a brief discussion and were allowed to take their good jet home to England. Their tanker waited in orbit while they shepherded their wingmen to Rota. This delay, along with the time spent waiting and searching for "Karma-52," caused some of the tankers to be low on fuel as the mission neared its end. As dawn approached, those KC-10s needing gas welcomed the arrival of KC-135s launched from England to cover this contingency. The big tankers refueled from their older smaller sister-ships while their respective coveys of F-111s watched from a comfortable distance.

The recovery of a single F-111F into Rota further revealed the very high political sensitivities associated with the raid. Even this minimal cooperation by the Spanish was not publicized until several weeks after the attack. But the low profile of the Spanish government was not observed in all quarters of the Spanish military. The day after the raid, a Spanish base commander summoned his resident American allies to an afternoon meeting at the officers' club. Not knowing what to expect, they arrived to discover a pleasant surprise: complimentary champagne and an enthusiastic toast, proposed by their host, to the United States Air Force![1]

Champagne was not on the menu awaiting the crews at Lakenheath. Coffee, pastries, and the traditional cold beer were what we had chosen to restore our exhausted, partially dehydrated pilots and WSOs. The crews were already reviving a bit as the sun continued to rise and daylight took hold. Despite the gray, misty English morning, they all felt the sense of well being brought on by seeing a sunrise which each of them had known they might miss.

But they still had to put their tired mounts safely on the ground before they could have their breakfast. The landing after any lengthy mission is a final, sometimes fatal, hazard. Unlike their Navy counterparts, for whom no landing is ever boring, Air Force pilots have to pump themselves up for the "routine" of landing. The night F-105 landings at Korat, Thailand, in the early '70s had required a quick Hershey bar and a wipe down with an iced wash cloth to ensure success—landing and stopping the speedy Thud on the sloping, bowed runway was very tricky. Fortunately, the much slower landing speed of the F-111 reduced the hazard to the 48th's returning aircrews. But, after fourteen hours aloft, no one could take the recovery portion of the mission for granted.

One by one, the Statue of Liberty Wing's ungainly Aardvarks descended through the thin overcast skies. As they passed through the last clouds at 1,000 feet of altitude, their landing lights became visible on final approach. On the flight line at Lakenheath, in a scene reminiscent of World War II, hundreds of the wing's people who had made the mission possible stood watching the skies, waiting for their jets and their friends to return. People from maintenance, munitions, the security police, and all of the many other organizations that had contributed to the raid's success were there. Despite the early hour, most now understood that this had been much more than an exercise. While many knew what had happened, there were few with any knowledge of the details. Had any airplanes been lost? If so, how many? Not many people knew how many jets remained airborne, but if they had they would have been hoping to count eighteen. Instead, they saw a total of sixteen landings during a period of over thirty minutes—of the attack force, only "Karma-52" and "Elton-43" had not returned to base. As the landings were taking place, the wives and children of "Karma-52"'s crew were learning for the first time that their husbands and fathers were missing in action.

As Major S. taxied toward the assigned hardened aircraft shelter, he watched the large number of waiting ground personnel in amazement, and felt a lump in his throat as he read their hand-lettered signs. He does not recall the exact wordings, but the primary sentiments expressed were "Welcome Home" and "Great Job—Well Done!" It would be several days before he understood that those feelings were shared by many millions of his countrymen. The Air Force's first mission in the war against terrorism was already being widely applauded by the American public. But the very negative reactions of Europeans would dominate the lives of all of us at Lakenheath for the immediate future.

At his TAB Vee (the widely used acronym/nickname for aircraft shelters: Theater Air Base Vulnerability shelter), Major S. was even more surprised to see several generals awaiting his arrival. Among them, the Air Force chief of staff General Gabriel stood out. Joining him were Lieutenant General Shaud and Major General McInerney. Unlike some of his fellow aviators, Major S. did not have to be helped from the cockpit, although the extended period of confinement did make his legs feel a bit unsteady as he saluted the approaching generals. After receiving their congratulations and handshakes and posing for a few personal pictures, Major S. attempted to answer General Gabriel's most interesting question: having gone into combat over both Hanoi and Tripoli, how would he compare their defenses? He evaluated Tripoli's defenses in this way: "On a scale of one-to-ten, the Triple-A was a five; on the same scale of one-to-ten, the missiles were a *fifteen!*" His less experienced buddies in the other F-111Fs undoubtedly shared his views on the latter. As he chatted with the top Air Force general, the last of those returning jets was touching down on Lakenheath's runway.

**APRIL 15–25, 1986**

**AFTERMATH**

As pointed out earlier, the same flag officers who would be greeting the returning aircrews later that morning had been assembled in the 48th Wing's command post at midnight, Greenwich mean time. Everyone on duty waited in an atmosphere of increasing tension as the clock ticked down to the mission's TOT. As April 15 arrived, we all eagerly awaited some initial word of the mission's success. Major General McInerney tried to ease the pervasive stress by talking acquisition with the chief. General Gabriel listened distractedly as McInerney espoused the merits of the British "ALARM" anti-radiation missile, and described how it could have been used that night if we had some in our inventory. While sharing his opinions on the missile and its use, I found it difficult to concentrate on the general's comments. Memories of tracers and SAM missile plumes reminded me of what our crews were facing at that moment. We all strained to hear the first radio calls that would indicate that our pilots and WSOs were safely homeward bound.

Minutes passed before those calls reached us, and even then the confusion that was taking place over the Mediterranean was being multiplied back in England. For a while it appeared very likely that two aircraft were missing; the confusion over call signs would not be corrected until after all the jets were back on their tankers. While the number of lost aircraft remained in question, the fact that at least one jet was missing became more and more certain as time passed. An hour after the raid ended, it was clear that the casualty notification apparatus we had set up would have to be used.

The command post had always had tight security during the mission, but at this point the level of attention to secrecy had to be raised another notch. I briefly reminded everyone on duty of our responsibilities. Those of us in the secure building were the only people who knew which pilot and WSO were missing. If word leaked out, the families could hear of the loss in a way that would be even more distressing for them. We would try our best to prevent that from happening.

Before 2 A.M., I gave the order to recall the people we had put on alert earlier—doctors, chaplains, and others—for a brief meeting that would determine how and when we would notify the affected families. While "how" was a relatively easy question to answer, "when" proved to be more difficult. Again, the raid's special circumstances contributed to the problem.

Around 3 A.M., General Donnelly telephoned from Ramstein. Was I aware, he asked, that the mission had been on live television in the U.S.? The mission's first bomb impacts had occurred in Qaddafi's Tripoli headquarters complex just as the Monday evening national news telecasts were beginning in the United States. Viewers of the nightly news programs had been startled to hear live descriptions of Tripoli under attack. If the excited commentary of reporters like NBC's Steve Delaney had not made the picture clear, the White House news conference featuring the Secretaries of State and Defense had certainly done so. Held less than three hours after the mission's time over target, this national broadcast had announced that F-111s based in England had conducted the raid, and that one of those aircraft was unaccounted for. General Donnelly informed me of this event, and asked if I understood the situation. Unaware of either the news telecasts or the press conference, I nevertheless caught the implication of what the general was saying. As the two of us were speaking, other telephone conversations were undoubtedly in progress between concerned friends or relatives and their loved ones in East Anglia. There was a definite chance that the families of our missing crew would find out about the loss of our jet in that manner, rather than through our official notification. Of course, the names of the pilot and WSO had not yet been revealed, so they would still be without the most critical information.

By 3 A.M., there were undoubtedly families of our aircrewmen who knew that an airplane was down, and were very worried about their particular pilot or WSO. We wanted to relieve their concerns as soon as possible by notifying the families of our missing crew. While General Donnelly encouraged me to consider immediate notification, he also stressed that it was my decision as to how and when it should be done. I thanked him for the information, and assured him that we would expedite this hated duty.

General Donnelly's caution was well founded in that the overseas phone calls to and from Lakenheath did begin during the early morning hours. By 5 A.M., BBC radio had also begun reporting that five aircraft had been lost on the raid—the wives who knew the mission was in progress fought back panic as they heard this exaggerated bulletin. By 6 A.M., squadron commanders' wives were making and receiving calls, trying to relieve the fears and passing on the rumors they had heard from unknown sources that only one airplane was down. The odds that one of the affected families would become involved in this informal notification process increased as the morning hours passed.

But, as a practical matter, several factors dictated against trying to dispatch a notification team to the homes of Mrs. Ribas-Do-minicci and Mrs. Lorence at 3 A.M. While all of the required people were now on duty, they were still unsure as to what had happened and what their response should be. In addition, both families lived off base in villages far from one another and from RAF Lakenheath. Two separate teams would be needed, both led by someone who had some idea of where to find the particular homes in question—no small feat on a black, misty English night. Just getting to the respective villages, Shipdham far to the northeast and Gazeley miles to the south near Newmarket, would take over thirty minutes in the dark. Considering all of this, the decision was made to send a team to each of the families arriving by 6:15 A.M. The time was chosen because it was near dawn and because it corresponded to the first morning news telecasts on British television. Popular with Americans, these news shows would offer the first probable source of notification, other than the stateside telephone calls over which we had no control. My wife and I would accompany one team and visit the other family later that morning, repeating a gut-wrenching duty we had first performed in California four years earlier.

At 5 A.M., we met with all the people involved in Colonel Westbrook's office. Joyce and I told them what we had experienced in 1982 hoping it would help; there were no questions since we all understood that no two people react the same way to such news. Each team was being led by a couple who were personal friends of the lost crewmen—they would help to cushion the blow as best they could. With everyone braced by coffee and our shared apprehension for the coming trauma, we piled into separate autos and drove off into the night.

Our small convoy of three cars ended up on a wild, hair-raising ride through the narrow byways of East Anglia. We had misjudged how long it would take to reach the Lorences' village of Shipdham, and our lead driver gradually built up speed as he raced to reach our destination before 6:15. We made it there just in time, and our persistent knocking eventually woke Paul's wife. Luckily, neither she nor Mrs. Ribas-Dominicci had been notified in any other way. But the fact that the official notification teams were the first to bring the sad news did not make it any easier.

Discovering that your beloved husband is MIA, missing in action off the coast of Libya, would be crushing news under any circumstances. When it comes out of the blue—after all, he said he was just flying in a peacetime local exercise—it is even more devastating. Neither surviving spouse had been given a chance to say goodbye.

We spent over an hour with Diana Lorence before Joyce and I excused ourselves to head for Gazeley to see Blanca Ribas-Dominicci. Both young women tried to make it easy on all of us by displaying the strength that their children would need in the years ahead. There were tears after initial incomprehension, but there were no breakdowns. The most uncomfortable moments came when either of them expressed their full faith in the ability of Paul or Fernando to survive and return. While the status of both pilot and WSO was officially MIA, the circumstances of their loss were such that it seemed unlikely that either could have survived. Without destroying all hope, we tried to gently make it clear to both wives that the odds were against them. They accepted or ignored our advice as they saw fit. Like all families who lose a loved one without the finality of burial or cremation, they suffered through the ensuing years with the shred of hope that accompanies continuing doubt. Unfortunately, the friends and family of Paul Lorence still live with that uncertainty as this book goes to press. Fernando's family received their deliverance with the return of his body in 1989.

After visiting both wives, we returned to Lakenheath as the last of the El Dorado Canyon task force was landing. The base's new status as the world's premier target for terrorist reprisals was already having an effect: guards with M-16 rifles checked every identification card at the main gate. As we headed for our quarters, we wondered what other problems we might encounter now that the bombing was over. The enormity of the raid's effects was anything but clear to us on the morning of April 15.

I headed for the 494 TFS building to join the debriefing process. The post-mission gathering there was a relatively low-key affair with the atmosphere of a party that would never reach its potential. The loss of Fernando and Paul hung over the crews. For many of them, their personal disappointment with the results they had achieved also dampened spirits. But despite these factors, the celebration you would expect on completing a first combat mission went on. It was increased by the dawning recognition that the mission they had flown had been anything but routine—"epic" seemed an apt description. The generally subdued hubbub included periodic cheers and exclamations as cockpit video- and audiotapes were reviewed. Pictures that within hours would be copied and televised worldwide found appreciative audiences in the 494th as mission crews judged their results and critiqued each other's weapons hits. General Gabriel and those accompanying him reviewed the tapes and, after further congratulating the surviving crews, began their return journey to the United States with copies of the selected bomb impacts to show to President Reagan. Major General McInerney stayed on, shaking the hand of every pilot and WSO and whispering "God bless you" to each. The process of debriefing, both formal and informal, eventually gave way to an unstructured bull session involving many who flew the mission and those who had not. Some of the flyers seemed reluctant to end the process: this had been their baptism by fire and they could not, or did not want to, stop talking about it.

Eventually exhaustion and the pressing need to see their families helped empty the 494th of El Dorado Canyon aircrews. The former did not bother many of them: they were too keyed up to really feel very tired. But exhaustion did send me home in a near-trance; a two-hour nap at noon was to be my first sleep in over thirty hours. As I drove across the base to my quarters, I began to consider just how different post-raid life at RAF Lakenheath would be. The implications of our attack on Tripoli were beginning to dawn on all who had taken part. The seriousness of the situation was probably best illustrated by the actions of one of the pilots.

Captain S. found his way home shortly before noon on April 15. The six-mile drive to the English village he had called home for almost two years was performed in a perfunctory manner as he listened to the BBC news broadcasts describing the mission. The extent of the coverage of the raid and its decidedly negative tone surprised him. As he walked through the door he had exited almost twenty-four hours earlier, he called out "Honey, I'm home" to his wife in the kitchen. She promptly burst into tears, greeting her husband gratefully as her fears for him finally evaporated. After a brief embrace, he turned wordlessly and proceeded to his work bench, where he found a claw hammer. She understood completely as he proceeded to the sign in front of his house. It named the home in the British tradition and, months earlier, he had added a family nameplate to show who lived there. He promptly tore it down in recognition of the fact that both he and his family had just become prime targets for terrorist retaliation. He was not the only American who took this action.

For those who had bombed Tripoli and for those who had supported their mission, the pleasant tranquil life of peacetime East Anglia had changed. The 48th TFW had conducted warfare against terrorists; it was not unreasonable to believe that terrorists would respond. And if they did respond, there was no assurance that they would strike against those who had made the decision to bomb—instead, they could very well decide to hit those who had done the bombing. The men and women in uniform did not like the possibility, but they understood and accepted that they were targets. What they could not accept easily was that their families were also at risk. In interviews, several of the mission's flyers recalled their feelings of relative helplessness during the weeks after the raid—they found it very hard to live with the threat to their loved ones and their inability to provide complete protection.

The 48th Wing's part in Operation El Dorado Canyon was unique in several respects, but none was more significant than the fact that it was launched from a "peacetime base" in peacetime. By a peacetime base, I mean one that, while equipped at all times to fly and fight, has not been able to take prudent actions in preparation for combat. Such actions would include evacuation of civilian dependents as hostilities approached; USAFE had plans for these evacuations, both to protect military spouses and children and to allow those in uniform to better perform their difficult combat jobs. For obvious reasons, both practical and political, it was impossible to issue such orders to the 48th Wing and the other supporting units in England. As a result, many crews who departed their quarters on Monday, April 14, left behind wives and children. They proceeded to fly history's longest fighter combat mission, and then returned to their sweethearts and "rug rats" on April 15. Those loved ones, along with their pilot and WSO husbands and fathers, promptly became targets for potential retaliation.

The reality of the threat was difficult to gauge, but the response at all levels told us that it was too real to be ignored. On April 15, the Air Force dispatched over two hundred additional security police to Europe. Some unknown number of them ended up at RAF Lakenheath, assisting our already locally augmented security police force in the daunting job of protecting our people and families on and off the base. As Secretary of Defense Caspar Weinberger had said that same day, "Military installations around the world are also on full alert for attacks—terrorist attacks of any kind from any quarter."[2] No unit anywhere had more reason to be concerned and alert than the Statue of Liberty Wing. Our people fully understood and took their security responsibilities seriously.

Security on any military installation is always visible, but seldom overbearing. There are guards at the gates and at important facilities for alert forces and weapons storage, and there are periodic planned or random patrols. With nearly one-fourth of our personnel involved in some manner, the weeks following the raid on Tripoli saw overwhelming security measures at RAF Lakenheath. Many cooks, clerks, and flight-line mechanics did double duty as combat-uniformed, fully armed security police. Their sheer numbers contributed to conflicting impressions of calm and danger. Their presence tended to make people feel more secure, while at the same time reminding everyone of the threat. Many who were there during the post-raid period cannot forget the pervasive atmosphere of dread that hung over U.S. bases in England in 1986. We had delivered a blow against terrorism with some degree of surprise; we steeled ourselves to receive a retaliatory blow "of any kind from any quarter." The fact that such an attack could prove successful despite our best security efforts added to the anxiety.

Still another factor that increased our concern was the quantity and quality of anti-U.S. media coverage in England and throughout Europe in the wake of the mission. Without AFN (Armed Forces Network) television or radio,[3] 48th Wing personnel were not immediately aware of the widespread support that the raid had in the United States. Instead, bombarded by a constant drumbeat of Qaddafi-inspired propaganda, they could be forgiven if they began to believe that the bombing mission against terrorism had been a terrible mistake. Initial English and European television coverage focused on the civilian casualties caused by the bombs mistakenly dropped near the French embassy. The first sentence in the lead editorial of the *Economist* issue of April 19 read in part, "In bombing Libya, the United States killed sleeping women and children and opened a dangerous new period." The death of an infant identified as Colonel Qaddafi's adopted daughter and his wife's tearful call for revenge also received widespread attention.[4] When not showing pictures of dead or injured Libyan civilians, the British and European media emphasized the results of various polls that indicated wide condemnation of the U.S. action against Qaddafi. Almost forgotten, it seemed, was the success of the raid against the selected military targets, as well as the series of heinous terrorist attacks dating back to 1985 that had prompted the bombing. We all felt regret for the unintentional killing of innocent civilians, but, as President Reagan later pointed out, we also regretted the deaths of innocent Americans in attacks conducted by Libyan-sponsored terrorists.

Perhaps these omissions were understandable; many Britons felt targeted and threatened in the aftermath of the raid. The Libyans had earlier shown a willingness to act irresponsibly in the U.K.: in 1984, the killing of a female London constable outside their embassy had outraged the English. Now they were to be subject to unpredictable Libyan acts of revenge—due primarily to U.S. government actions. Some Labour party politicians seized on the comparison that the "only crime" of the dead Libyan civilians was that they had lived too close to military installations—like their counterparts in East Anglia perhaps![5]

It had been fairly easy to predict a visceral anti-American reaction after the mission. In the days preceding the attack, British media had publicized a contentious debate about whether the U.S. could launch such a raid without the permission of Her Majesty's government. The consensus seemed to be that the Status of Forces agreement between the U.S. and the U.K., or at least that part of it which is not highly secret, was so vague that it did not specifically preclude us from doing so. Therefore, it was at least possible that President Reagan, the "shoot-first-and-ask-questions-later" cowboy portrayed by the British left, could employ U.S. military forces from England in any manner he wished. The chance of that prompted harsh criticism of the Tories for having permitted the British Isles to become a large, permanent American aircraft carrier.

While all of this was interesting to those of us at Lakenheath, the internal British debate was of real concern in only one specific respect. If the U.S. had, in fact, acted unilaterally without Mrs. Thatcher's permission, the anti-American reaction could have been explosive. The pre-raid speculation that such permission would not be given heightened our concerns as the bombs fell on Tripoli. As things turned out, we on the scene were not aware of the British government's cooperation with the raid until the first news reports were made on April 15. That knowledge helped in two ways: first, we knew that the expected protests would be easier to manage. And second and much more important, we could expect the full cooperation of all British security agencies in coping with the problem of possible revenge attacks.

While local Suffolk newspapers sported headlines like "Fears of Revenge Attacks," and the BBC reminded us that a full two-thirds of Britons were against the raid, the first demonstrators against the mission began appearing around RAF Lakenheath and nearby RAF Mildenhall.[6] Within forty-eight hours of the raid, small groups of CND supporters were involved in picketing both bases. Several thousand gathered in London near the Ministry of Defense, and hundreds were arrested. Their fears of reprisal against themselves and the 5,000 Britons living in Libya gained credence as various terrorist actions rippled across the globe. The most blatant attacks included an American being shot and critically wounded in Khartoum, three hostages (two British and one American) being executed by their captors in Beirut, and a near-tragedy involving an attempt to bomb an airliner departing from London's Heathrow airport. The latter involved a pregnant Irishwoman who was duped into carrying a hidden bomb onboard an El Al jetliner by her Palestinian lover; only the extra layers of Israeli airline security prevented this attack from being successful.

These events helped to swell the crowd at a planned major demonstration at RAF Lakenheath on Sunday, April 20, to almost 2,000 protestors. Marching along a roadway known as Lord's Walk on the main base's southern border, this peaceful but noisy protest disrupted traffic on and around the airbase for several hours. The protestors, many from the CND, carried signs with messages against the raid, Mrs. Thatcher, President Reagan, and the presence of U.S. military forces in their country. The cries of "Yanks, Go Home" reminded me that Americans had not been totally welcome here even during World War II. My uncle's final B-17 mission had taken off from a field less than thirty miles away—perhaps he had encountered similar, but less visible, resentment in 1943. In any case, most of us watched the demonstration from a distance with curiosity and some apprehension. Colonel Westbrook had alerted the wing to possible problems through a bulletin issued on April 18. In it, he warned of contact with the protestors that could turn into a confrontation or an incident, and reminded us that we served in an alliance "dedicated to preserving the citizen's right to freely express opinions." At Sam's urging, most Lakenheath Americans stayed out of sight, and the demonstration quietly broke up around nightfall.

Fortunately, the opinions emanating from the CND were not the only British voices being heard. Members of the Conservative party rallied to the defense of Mrs. Thatcher's decision and the U.S. action. To regain perspective, one local MP (Member of Parliament), Sir Eldon Griffiths of Bury St. Edmunds, suggested that East Anglians remember that "we have been on the front line in this area for a very long time."[7] He also chastised the left for spreading fear and hysteria. Sir Eldon warned that "to suggest that blood is going to run in the streets of Suffolk is the height of irresponsibility." His advice to keep cool and look at the facts would eventually bear fruit; as time passed, a significant percentage of our British neighbors changed their minds, regarding the mission more favorably and accepting the threat of terrorist retaliation with traditional British resolve. But in the days immediately after the raid, even we Americans could not fully share Sir Eldon's optimism.

After all, we were trying to return to the normalcy of peacetime while armed security police escorted our children to and from school and stood guard in our back yards. It was a stress-producing, surreal experience that contributed to a growing sense of gloom for some. The wing's dependents, unprepared for the post-mission trauma beforehand, now found themselves receiving belated advice and assistance. Anti-terrorism briefings urged them to be alert, to change their normal daily routines, to do whatever they could do to make themselves less tempting targets. Families and friends of the pilots and WSOs who flew the mission were urged to keep their names secret—the threat of direct reprisals against the crews and their families was emphasized. That threat remains very real to several of them even today, over five years after the mission. In researching this book, I found some crewmen who politely declined my offer to cooperate. I also found no one who disagreed with the decision to keep their names out of print.

The most practical among us could not help but realize that even our best efforts might not succeed in deterring or disrupting a well-planned terrorist action. Perhaps we would have been more at ease had we understood all of the actions, both open and secret, that the British government was taking to protect its citizens and their American guests. The seriousness of the situation had been fully demonstrated by the attempted El Al bombing within days of the raid; the foiling of this terrorist attempt had served to heighten everyone's awareness. The British security efforts, in full cooperation with our own security apparatus, would ultimately prove successful. One particular example of quick decisive action on our behalf illustrates how the British handled potential terrorists.

As the raid took place, over two hundred Libyan pilots were undergoing training at a base outside London. Slated for the Libyan national airline after graduation, these young men were understandably disturbed by the bombing of their national capital. Nevertheless, they were probably not considered a major threat until one of them, in a monitored telephone conversation with friends or relatives in Libya, revealed his status as a volunteer to take a light plane on a one-way suicide revenge mission against an American airbase. RAF Upper Heyford, where the EF-111 Ravens or Sparkvarks that supported El Dorado Canyon were based, was less than thirty miles distant. Lakenheath itself was within thirty minutes' flying time. The circumstances exposed by this chance conversation were too serious to ignore: the British government acted within hours to deport the pilot in question and eleven other Libyan students deemed high-risk by British security.[8] To this day, the state of training of today's Libyan airline pilot is a matter of concern to me. But in 1986, their prompt removal from the U.K. was just one of a series of actions that made all 12,000 Americans in the RAF Lakenheath community breathe easier.

Other nations were also beginning to move against Libya's interests, though belatedly. U.S. calls for such cooperation to rein in Qaddafi during the months leading up to the raid had gone unanswered, except for a last-gasp European Community communique issued on the day of the raid's execution. Now, after the bombing, Europe finally initiated some concerted political and economic action against state-sponsored terrorism. Libyan diplomats were expelled from West Germany, Spain, and Denmark in the weeks following the raid. Throughout Europe, governments took action to restrict the personnel manning the Libyan People's Bureaus, putting them under observation or imposing new travel restrictions to reduce their capability to support terrorist activities. As *Newsweek* reported on April 28, European intelligence agencies that traditionally do not talk to one another began cooperating in the raid's aftermath. The overall effect was an unprecedented, unified campaign to discourage terrorism. Our "embarrassed and enraged" allies, to use *Newsweek*'s description, began to reap the very real rewards of the mission within hours of its execution, but it took time for most of them to recognize those benefits. Nevertheless, some saw the real state of things immediately: a small U.S. Air Force contingent on duty in Scotland discovered this fact the day following the bombing. In civilian clothes and visiting a small pub for their dinner and a pint, they were asked by the locals if they had anything to do with the United States Air Force. Admitting their membership in same, they were surprised to find the next round of ale being bought by their enthusiastic hosts.[9] It appears that, privately at least, many throughout Europe and even in the Arab world shared their views.

Such private displays of support were not helping much at Lakenheath. Colonel Westbrook decided within days that the steady
bombardment of criticism in the British media had to be coun-
tered. Working with the base's public affairs specialists, he requested digests of printed news coverage from the United States
and videotapes of U.S. telecasts. These were promptly duplicated
and distributed for the benefit of our troops and their dependents.
The wide dissemination of these materials helped dispel the impression, easily gained from the BBC, that the wing had commit-
ted a war crime. Instead, Statue of Liberty Wing members
discovered that their countrymen enthusiastically supported the
raid. Results of initial public opinion polls were almost exactly
opposite those taken in Europe: nearly three out of four Americans approved of the raid. This happy news helped unit and individual morale despite the continuing stress of staying on guard
against terrorist reprisal.

Support for the wing in the U.S. also took more tangible
forms. One strong enthusiast for our efforts was H. Ross Perot,
the Texas millionaire who had strong ties to all branches of the
military. Mr. Perot was so impressed by the raid that he quickly
offered to host a party in honor of the aviators who had flown
the mission. Both Air Force headquarters and the wing saw flaws
in the first proposed plan for the party: an all-American, full dress
party at a posh London hotel would undoubtedly attract British
protestors, Libyan terrorists, or a combination of both. Eventually, the Pentagon approved a plan that became a reality: H. Ross
Perot footed the bill for the huge 1986 Fourth of July picnic at
RAF Lakenheath. His contributions produced a wonderful day
for the wing; just one more indication of how their fellow countrymen viewed the April mission.

Colonel Westbrook also took quick action to deal with the
problem of stress mentioned earlier. Commanders and supervi-
sors received guidance on what stress reactions they might expect
to see and how to deal with them. Individuals were encouraged
to discuss their concerns openly in order to dilute the impact on
any one person. The wing also established a twenty-four-hour
rumor control hot line so that some of the wilder speculations
that would predictably surface could be quickly submerged. The
hot line functioned throughout the weekend protests following

the raid, and was eventually shut down several days later as the situation stabilized. All in all, Colonel Westbrook's efforts to keep the wing on an even keel under very difficult circumstances were successful. Those who needed help got it; those who were not worried continued along, unfazed by the whole affair.

Some of these latter folks were undoubtedly the source of the black humor that began to surface at Lakenheath, seemingly within hours of the mission. It is important to realize that, despite the strained post-raid atmosphere, many of our people were anything but depressed by what had happened. Instead, they rightfully felt that they had executed the major part of a historic combat mission, the first such USAF mission in over a dozen years. And, for the most part as detailed in a later chapter of this book, the raid had been a success. In the spirit that has marked U.S. fighting units throughout our nation's history, the men and women of the 48th Wing reacted to a tough situation with a sense of humor. Patches for the "Winner" of the "NORTH AF-RICA BOMB COMP[etition] '86" began appearing shortly after the raid. Even quicker on the scene were the T-shirts and baseball caps suggesting that L.I.B.Y.A. stood for

Lakenheath
Is
Bombing
Your
Ass

In addition to the locally generated humor, the wing commander's mail bag sometimes contained materials that lightened the moment. In the weeks following the raid, Colonel Westbrook received mail sent directly to the wing from all over the world. In general, the letters reflected U.S. public opinion trends in that they were overwhelmingly favorable towards the mission. A typical letter thanked the wing for its professionalism and courage, and complimented us for doing a dirty job very well under difficult circumstances. But not all of this correspondence had a serious tone, as evidenced by the greeting card we received from a gentleman in Cornwall. Hand-made, the card's cover shouted in living color, "STOP DROPPING BOMBS ON MISTER QAD-DAFI!" Inside, it suggested that we should do all Britons a favor and "DROP THAT SILLY CND MOB ON THE BASTARD INSTEAD." Constrained from entering into British political matters, we decided not to follow up on this recommendation.

On the other hand, U.S. politics were also represented in our mail. Colonel Westbrook was addressed by name in one letter that arrived in a high quality, heavy bond envelope with a return address of 1600 Pennsylvania Avenue. The official-looking document inside began, "Dear Sam: I covered your ass this time, but if you *ever* launch another unauthorized raid on Libya . . . ." At the time, I was certain that this letter, supposedly from President Reagan, was an elaborate practical joke. (Years later, revelations concerning the planning and decision-making role of Marine Corps Lt. Col. Oliver North in Operation El Dorado Canyon would briefly make me wonder.)[10] Fortunately, the known facts favor the conclusion that the president made the final decision on the bombing of Libya in 1986.

As indicated, the atmosphere around RAF Lakenheath after the raid was a decidedly mixed bag, but if one emotion was predominant it had to be mourning. The declaration of the crew as MIA the night of the raid had been only temporary. Under the circumstances, the unit commander has the duty and authority to declare the missing men KIA, killed in action, if the weight of evidence supports that determination. Colonel Westbrook quickly came to the conclusion that this action was justified: post-mission search and rescue efforts had found no evidence that either crewman had survived. Their failure to immediately appear on Libyan television broadcasts was more convincing evidence that they were not alive; there was little doubt that Colonel Qaddafi would have used prisoners for propaganda had he taken any. Within days of the attack, the wives and families were gently given the news that their husbands and fathers would not be returning. This decision led to plans for an appropriate memorial service, which was held in a hangar on the base one week after the raid on Monday, April 21.

My wife and I would miss the memorial service for Maj. Fernando Ribas-Dominicci and Capt. Paul Lorence due to military orders. On Sunday night, after the anti-American protest had broken up outside RAF Lakenheath, we drove to Felixstowe to take the ferry to Zeebrugge, Belgium, en route to USAFE headquarters at Ramstein. For the next week, I would be serving as a member of a below-the-zone board, selecting lieutenant colonel candidates for early promotion to colonel. In this role, I would be helping to determine the fate of many other officers. My own fate would be decided in my absence.

The memorial service at Lakenheath drew a respectful, overflowing crowd that came to honor the two men who had failed to return from the mission. The tributes they received included a moving speech by the U.S. ambassador to the U.K., Charles H. Price II. Ambassador Price and the other speakers cited the courage, discipline, and devotion that had characterized the lives of the lost aviators. The ceremony concluded with a missing man flyby, the traditional Air Force salute to lost comrades. Almost as soon as the service ended, a related controversy began, centering on a seemingly simple question: which medals would be appropriate to honor both the deceased crewmen and the surviving Libyan raiders? As this book is published, despite the official view of the U.S. Air Force, that controversy is still very much alive and well.

April 16, 1985: F-111F, tail # 416, off the RAF Lakenheath runway due to a blown tire. Captain Fernando Ribas-Dominicci, killed in action one year later on the raid, was the pilot involved in this incident. *(Courtesy of P. Shaw)*

September 12, 1985: Prince Charles visits Lakenheath and the Statue of Liberty Wing. As viewed, the prince is flanked on the left by Colonel Sam Westbrook and on the right by Major General Thomas McInerney. The author is seated between the general and Colonel Tom Yax, 48th TFW/DO, under the flag of the Royal Air Force. *(Author's Collection)*

Miss Liberty: The Statue of Liberty Wing was and is the only Air Force unit with both a number and a name. This miniature Miss Liberty was a gift to the wing from the people of Chaumont, France. She stands proudly in a small traffic circle near the RAF Lakenheath base hospital. (*U.S. Air Force*)

Exercise in Progress: For over forty years, exercises like these were as close as any U.S. fighter wing in Europe came to real combat. The raid on Libya is the only instance in which combat operations were conducted from a unit's home base. Note the full chemical defense ensembles. (*U.S. Air Force*)

The command post's "Battle Cab." Colonel Westbrook mans the position he assigned to the author for Operation El Dorado Canyon. This was also the site of the discussion of the "twenty-hour option" detailed in chapter 4. (*U.S. Air Force*)

March 1986: F-111F, tail #
389, on a training sortie from
Incirlik air base in Turkey.
This photo, taken approximately three weeks before the
mission, is the last known picture of the aircraft lost in the
attack on Tripoli. *(Courtesy of
G. Coker)*

April 14, 1986: An F-111F en route to Libya on the night of the raid, taking fuel from a KC-10 tanker. This is one of the ill-fated "Karma" element—possibly "Karma-52," the aircraft that was lost. Not one of the three planes in this element was successful in its attack on Colonel Qaddafi's headquarters at Azziziyah Barracks. *(Courtesy of Lt. Col. C. Hale)*

April 15, 1986: An F-111F with empty weapons pylons, thought to be "Karma-51," tail # 413, returning to England after bombing Qaddafi's capital. *(Courtesy of Lt. Col. C. Hale)*

April 15, 1986: The unidentified crew of the KC-10 tanker "Debar-88," tail # 1710, safely back on British soil after supporting the operation. Many tanker crews reached England just hours before the actual mission. *(Courtesy of Lt. Col. C. Hale)*

May 1986: Colonel Westbrook, the author, and several unidentified 48th TFW personnel pose for a publicity still for the July 1986 issue of *Life* magazine. To date, none of the Air Force crewmen who bombed Libya have been publicly identified. *(Author's Collection)*

# RECOGNITION

Making a spontaneous assessment immediately after the mission, Major General McInerney commented that, someday, the men who had flown the F-111Fs in Operation El Dorado Canyon would be remembered in the same way as General Doolittle's Tokyo Raiders. I share that view, and hope that this book will help achieve that deserved recognition. However, the events that developed in the weeks and months after the mission proved that many people did not share General McInerney's opinion. Indeed, the overall level of recognition provided to the wing and to the people who flew the mission points to a conscious decision to downplay the raid on Qaddafi's Libya.

The subject of awards for any combat operation is inherently controversial and, in peacetime at least, political. If generals do not actually plan for the last war, they at least consider it strongly in determining awards and decorations for the next war. For that reason, writing about the subject in 1991, in the aftermath of Desert Storm and its unprecedented aerial bombardment campaign against Iraq, is difficult. To some extent, the reader must try to consider the topic of awards for El Dorado Canyon in isolation from other previous or subsequent military operations. Of course, that is the way that such awards are supposed to be determined: strictly on the basis of the facts in each individual instance. Unfortunately, in the wake of the Grenada invasion of 1983, that does not seem to have been done in 1986.

Recognition for the wing was one of the matters to be decided after the mission. Colonel Westbrook made the decision to nominate the 48th Wing for the Presidential Unit Citation (PUC). This award is designed to recognize outstanding achievements by any organization, large or small, although the typical Air Force recipient in the past has been a wing in combat. Sam was considering every aspect of the mission when he made this recommendation. The fact that the wing had operated under sustained pressure for over three months was part of it. The fact that the wing had successfully adapted to the amazing turbulence caused by the major late changes to the plan was also considered. Finally, the record length and complexity of the night raid, as well as its success in damaging all three assigned targets, pointed to wing-wide recognition as an appropriate goal. Sam submitted the recommendation expecting that it would get a full and fair hearing and would probably be approved. He had already departed for his new assignment as the commandant of cadets at the U.S. Air Force Academy in Colorado when we discovered that the Air Force had other ideas.

When awarded to a unit, the Presidential Unit Citation is normally given to everyone assigned to that unit during the time of the outstanding performance. People assigned to the unit later may wear the distinctive ribbon only during their tour of duty with the cited organization. When the eventual Air Force decision regarding the PUC was made, neither Sam Westbrook nor his successor, Col. Tom Barber, could understand it or live with it. It proposed that portions of the wing (the command section, the tactical fighter squadrons, most of the maintenance complex, etc.) should receive the award, while other parts of the wing (the logistics complex, the personnel shop, individuals within wing headquarters such as the attorneys, etc.) would be denied the award.

A fighter wing is an entity that produces combat power, with all of its varied elements contributing directly or indirectly to that goal. That combat power is measured in terms of sorties produced in a given time period, but a wise commander cannot limit his appraisal of his organization only to those who are directly involved in launching, flying, and recovering the jets. Every man and woman in a wing does his or her job and, in so doing, makes the wing succeed or fail. If someone attempts to draw lines between major and minor contributors, they are bound to make mistakes. Worse, their effort drives a wedge into an otherwise cohesive unit, designating some as essential and others as ancillary. An Air Force tactical fighter wing is just as much a fighting unit as is any Navy carrier—only the physical layout of the organization is different. For reasons that escaped me and defied logic and precedence, the Air Force did not see it that way after El Dorado Canyon.

Tom Barber eventually took the only tenable position for a wing commander in this situation—he withdrew the wing's nomination for the award. Rather than drive a stake into the heart of the wing by having some members receive the PUC while others were denied it, he chose to turn down the award for any of the 48th's people. As this is written, the only unit commendation the 48th TFW has been awarded for El Dorado Canyon came from the U.S. Navy!

There are three noteworthy footnotes regarding unit awards given to the 48th Wing for Operation El Dorado Canyon. The first is worth noting if for no other reason than its entertainment value. On September 7, 1986, the then Secretary of the Navy John F. Lehman visited Lakenheath. The highlight of his visit occurred when he surprised the wing and the Air Force by presenting the wing commander with the Navy Meritorious Unit Citation for its role in the mission. It was the first unilateral interservice presentation of this award in the history of the Navy, and it promptly ended any argument or controversy over the PUC mentioned earlier in these pages. Months later, General Donnelly would note that the Department of Defense had made the decision to go with the Navy medal and withdraw the PUC since no unit can receive two awards for the same action.[1] Based on my knowledge of the situation, this interpretation is probably correct as far as it goes, but falls far short of explaining the problems surrounding the PUC nomination detailed here. In any case, the men and women who served at Lakenheath between April 10 and 16, 1986, proudly wear their Navy Meritorious Unit Citations. In what can only be considered a major embarrassment to the Air Force, this was the only award the wing was really offered.

The second footnote has to do with the curious determination, made by organizations like *Aviation Week & Space Technology* magazine, that the mission deserved no overall recognition. That prestigious aviation publication saw insufficient merit in the mission to include it in its annual "Laurels" award program. *Aviation Week* instead cited the same mission that eventually won the Mackay Trophy in their "Laurels for 1986" column along with an F-16 pilot who landed his crippled electric jet at Glenview NAS outside Chicago.[2] As a matter of interest, only the Air Force Association saw fit to honor the mission with an award, presenting the David C. Schilling Award for outstanding contribution in the field of flight to the Operation El Dorado Canyon task force as a whole.

The final footnote on unit awards deals with the previously mentioned Mackay Trophy itself. The Air Force has an annual program for recognizing outstanding feats of aviation. The program encompasses a number of prestigious, traditional awards, some of which date back to the early days of military flying. In 1987, by coincidence I had the honor of serving as the president of the board of officers who selected the individual and unit winners for the Air Force awards for 1986. We also selected Air Force nominees for awards given by other organizations to all the services.

It surprised me to discover that the 48th TFW had not been nominated to receive the Mackay Trophy for "the most meritorious flight of the year" for 1986. The award, also "for gallantry and intrepidity," seemed to be perfectly appropriate for the wing that had been the core of a historic one-time combat mission. While the other nominees, including the eventual winning KC-10 flight crew, were certainly deserving, I directed an inquiry to USAFE headquarters to ensure that an oversight had not occurred. The answer came back within hours: neither the wing nor Third Air Force had nominated the 48th for the award, and nobody in the headquarters at Ramstein had considered doing it either.

As to individual awards, the story is, if anything, even more difficult to understand. However, before beginning this discussion, the difficulties involved in *publicly* recognizing the crews who flew the mission should be acknowledged. Obviously, each of these men was and is subject to possible reprisals from terrorists, a factor which is still involved in the writing of this book and the decision not to name any of them over five years later. However, one crew was beyond reprisals even in 1986, and we moved quickly to give them the recognition we were certain they had earned. Immediately after the mission, Colonel Westbrook decided to nominate the three flight leaders for the Distinguished Flying Cross, all other surviving crewmen for the Air Medal, and Captains Ribas-Dominicci and Lorence for the prestigious Silver Star. Only the decision on the posthumous awards required fast action: it was hoped that these awards could be approved quickly and presented to the bereaved families within weeks. With that in mind, and with full knowledge of the situation that had faced Fernando and Paul on their first combat mission, Colonel Westbrook opted to use the message format for Silver Star nominations. This procedure, as outlined in the governing Air Force regulation, allows the nomination to go out by message directly to the secretary of the Air Force, with intermediate headquarters required to vote "Yea" or "Nay" by message within a specified time. Informal contact with Third Air Force headquarters pointed to early approval from that quarter, but similar contact with the command's personnel staff at the headquarters in Ramstein, Germany, gave the first indications of trouble.

It seems that the wing's position conflicted with a "talking paper" on likely awards and decorations for El Dorado Canyon produced by the USAFE personnel staff at the request of the USAFE chief of staff. During my promotion board duty at Ramstein less than two weeks after the raid, I had seen a draft of this paper. Produced in isolation from the realities of the mission and reflecting political imperatives which I will explain later, it had apparently already been accepted as the "command position"—before Colonel Westbrook's message nominations reached Germany. As a result, we at Lakenheath were shocked to receive a one-sentence message, signed by the USAFE chief of staff, telling the secretary of the Air Force that USAFE headquarters disagreed with the Silver Star nominations for our two dead comrades. At the same time, the concurring message from Third Air Force never developed; by then, the controversial nature of the subject had become known in Major General McInerney's headquarters, and the earlier assurances of support had changed to prudent silence.

This development left Sam Westbrook, by now absorbed in the preparations for his departure for Colorado, in the unenviable position of having inadvertently embarrassed our higher head-quarters at Ramstein. At least that was the view that seemed to prevail above the wing—no one outwardly shared our view that it was very embarrassing for the Air Force, at any level, to be openly opposing high posthumous awards for the only two fighter crewmen to have died in combat in over a decade. In any case, the immediate result of USAFE's action was that Silver Stars were not to be presented to the grieving families, and the wing went back to the drawing board in its attempt to justify those awards for the mission's only casualties.

A subsequent attempt to nominate Major (posthumously pro-moted) Ribas-Dominicci and Captain Lorence for Silver Stars was also unsuccessful. The wing produced, and Third Air Force modified and endorsed nomination packages that pro-vided significant detail concerning the mission and the hurdles that had faced these officers. Despite this information, USAFE stuck to its original staff position, and downgraded the awards, not to the next lowest award, the Distinguished Flying Cross, but to the same Air Medal that the surviving crewmembers received.

Why were we so certain that posthumous Silver Stars were justified? First of all, the tripling in the size of the F-111F attack force meant that many crews had less than seventy-two hours to prepare for the mission. Fernando and Paul were among those crewmen who had very limited time to get ready for the raid. They were also one of the three crews who had the added burden of knowing that they were attacking from positions that were known to be significantly more dangerous than the others. They were well aware that their immediate superiors had recom-mended against flying nine aircraft over the most heavily de-fended target. They also knew that the wing leadership had been overruled on that matter. As knowledgeable tacticians in their own right, they had come to their own conclusions on the viabil-ity of their attack positions before the final briefings began. And, during those final briefings, an Air Force two-star general had publicly acknowledged that their three-ship element would face great hazards.

What did the men involved think of all this? No one will ever know for certain, but the actions of one of them prior to takeoff may give some indication. Captain Ribas-Dominicci, a devout Roman Catholic, sought out Father Higgins, one of our Catholic chaplains, and asked to go to confession and receive communion. Fernando's special effort to take part in these sacraments seems indicative of a man who knew the hazards he faced—and wanted to be certain that all was in order, spiritually and in every other way, before he undertook this mission. It is possible to come to other conclusions about his state of mind, but the reader should try to put himself or herself in his position, knowing the things he knew, when he went looking for the chaplain. It is difficult to believe that any of the six men flying in the last three positions against Qaddafi's headquarters were sanguine about their chances. Most, including Fernando and Paul, were flying their first combat mission. It would be the longest flight any of them had ever made, and it would be done at night. Finally, they would be engaged by the most technologically sophisticated defenses faced by the U.S. Air Force up to that time; and those defenses would be fully alerted well before they came into range.

Yet they pressed on, doing their jobs for the six-plus hours it took them to reach the target area, especially during the last few minutes when, up ahead, their buddies' screaming F-111s dropped the bombs that would serve to further alert the Libyans. Not one of these three crews was successful in putting bombs on the preplanned targets, but "Karma-52," Fernando and Paul, came close. Still over water and with less than a minute to bomb release, "Karma-52" was traveling through a volley of surface-to-air missiles under the eerie glow of unexpected flares fired from boats in the harbor. While a heavy volume of conventional anti-aircraft fire was also in progress, "Karma-52" was still out of range of the spectacular light show being put on by the excited Libyan gunners. As previously stated, the evidence available today indicates that they were probably hit by a missile and then ejected too late from their crippled aircraft.

In the author's view, the question is not, Were the Silver Star nominations justified? The question is, Are posthumous Silver Stars *still* justified for Major Ribas-Dominicci and Captain Lorence? Various acts of courage in war sometimes take years or decades to get the recognition they deserve. As I write these words, I remain hopeful that this subject can be revived within the Air Force, and that the previous decisions can be reversed. If and when that happens, the U.S. dead of El Dorado Canyon will have finally been given their country's just reward.

Responding to an article in the December 8, 1986, issue of *Defense Week* that noted the controversy, General Donnelly, still CINCUSAFE at the time, wrote that he had not recommended approval of the Silver Stars for Fernando and Paul "based solely on the criteria for the award." He also noted that the officers had each received the following posthumous awards: the Air Medal, the Purple Heart, and the Meritorious Service Medal.[3]

Discussion of these three awards, in keeping with Air Force thoughts on recognition for El Dorado Canyon, should probably be done in reverse order. First, the Meritorious Service Medal: this medal is normally presented in peacetime as an end-of-tour decoration for a company or field grade officer or relatively senior NCO who has successfully completed his or her assignment with above average achievement and no black marks. According to the *Air Force Times*, the U.S. Air Force presented 23,443 Meritorious Service Medals in 1986.[4]

As to the Purple Heart, this award is automatically presented to any American killed or wounded in action during combat operations. While the automatic nature of the award is explanation in and of itself why this award is insufficient to recognize gallantry, the recent history of the Purple Heart should also be considered. Yes, this violates the suggestion that the acts of courage and achievement on Operation El Dorado Canyon should be reviewed in isolation, but the facts in this instance are too compelling to ignore. In a move that has surely come back to haunt the service that in 1990 deployed roughly twenty percent of its strength to the deserts of Saudi Arabia, it has been reported that the U.S. Army presented the Purple Heart to at least one soldier who suffered only from heat stroke during 1989's Operation Just Cause in Panama![5]

The Air Medal deserves a more detailed discussion. In 1986, the Air Force presented 3,849 Air Medals to its members.[6] Some were obviously harder earned than others. Only a few dozen were for performance in combat, and only two of those were for acts of courage in the line of fire that, in the opinion of many, were an order of magnitude greater than the rest. What sort of activity earned an Air Medal besides dying for your country? While not conversant with the detailed criteria used in 1986, I can list several examples from previous experience. Crewmen have been awarded the Air Medal for completing twenty peacetime AWACS missions while in Saudi Arabia. Others have received Air Medals for successfully intercepting Soviet bomber aircraft a given number of times, typically ten or fifteen. Finally, there are reports of non-aircrew engineers getting the Air Medal for some number of sorties aboard research and development aircraft like the airborne laser laboratory. The bottom line is that none of these activities involve any exposure to enemy fire; the threat of possible danger has been and is today considered sufficient to earn an Air Medal. How else could the Air Force justify over 3,000 awards in a year of peace (another 3,350 were doled out in 1987)?

In the opinion of many in the Air Force, including every El Dorado Canyon aircrewman I have contacted, awarding the Air Medal to Major Ribas-Dominicci and Captain Lorence as the highest award earned on their final mission was ludicrous at best, shameful at worst. And, as will be seen, the men and women of the Statue of Liberty Wing were not the only ones to challenge this action.

General Donnelly, as indicated earlier, cited the criteria for the Silver Star as his only consideration in recommending disapproval. A brief paraphrase of the award's requirements is that it can only be given to those who have demonstrated gallantry in action while engaged in operations against an enemy of the United States or an opposing foreign force. "Gallantry in action" is further defined by the governing regulation as "heroism of high degree involving risk of life." The actions taken by Fernando and Paul that night would seem to justify the conclusion that they met and exceeded that criterion.

Prior to my retirement from the service less than sixteen months after the mission, I made two efforts to gain reconsideration for these two Silver Star nominations.[7] The first was through a classified letter to General Donnelly which was never answered. The second was through a similar, unclassified letter in 1987 to his successor, Gen. William Kirk, which did prompt a reply. General Kirk's chief of staff, a major general, wrote that there was insufficient evidence available to prompt a reversal of General Donnelly's 1986 decision. The rationale was consistent with that used to reply to other interested parties in 1989.

By that year, at the urging of the family of Fernando Ribas-Dominicci, the governor of Puerto Rico wrote to the then Air Force chief of staff, Gen. Larry D. Welch, petitioning the service for a reversal of the decision against the Silver Star. The Ribas-Dominicci family, while pleased with various actions taken on his and their behalf (naming a street for him at a training base; congressional action on behalf of his son), understood the implications of the lesser award for Fernando. While not knowing why, they recognized that Air Force leadership did not seem to hold his sacrifice in as high esteem as they might have. Governor Rafael Hernandez Colon's request of February 1989 followed the service's dismissal of a resolution by the Senate of the Commonwealth of Puerto Rico that advocated the same action. In both instances, General Welch's negative replies cited the many other awards given Fernando, and indicated that the commander on the scene had personally made the decision against the award based on existing criteria.[8]

The telling point, mentioned by General Welch to justify not changing the decision and cited earlier by General Kirk's staff, was the fact that the commander in the field had personally evaluated the situation and had made the decision. The correspondence from both headquarters, USAFE in Ramstein and USAF headquarters in Washington, reveals a very strong reluctance to reverse the decision of an on-scene commander. That attitude is indicative of an even stronger institutional reluctance on the part of the exclusive club of Air Force four-star generals to find fault with the decision of any club member. A footnote to this discussion is that the only real defender of the decisions regarding awards and decorations for the dead crew has been Gen. Charles L. Donnelly, the man who has been credited by some with the decision that overruled the wing and sent three extra jets against the most heavily defended target. Heaping high praise and posthumous awards for courage on those who have attempted to execute a flawed plan could be considered an effort to compensate for the fact that the plan was faulty. Moreover, faced with a similar situation, there are many who would probably make decisions identical to those of General Donnelly.

No callousness or malicious intended is implied by this discussion. It is easy to understand why a person in General Donnelly's position would choose the course he selected with regard to El Dorado Canyon awards and decorations. He was an extremely busy man in a position of great responsibility; his staff made a flawed recommendation which he was predisposed to accept; and he did not have all of the pertinent information at his disposal when he initially faced the decision. But why did the USAFE staff adopt the stance they selected?

While no one can be certain, one factor seems to have played a major role. In 1983, both the Air Force and the Army had suffered major public relations damage after the Grenada awards fiasco—almost 9,000 medals had been distributed in the weeks immediately after an operation with only 7,000 participants. In the spring of 1986, the recommendation of General Donnelly's staff, drafted and adopted as the USAFE position within days of the raid and in isolation from many pertinent facts known only at Lakenheath, reached him at a time when the subject of combat awards was undoubtedly still controversial. The USAFE staff, leaning far away from the post-Grenada controversy, had given him a seemingly unassailable position—the Air Force would generate no new criticism for being overly generous with its medals.

The very human tendency to attribute failure to others, in this case evidenced by the loss of a single combat aircraft, may have also come into play. Adm. William Crowe, chairman of the Joint Chiefs of Staff, had said that the possibility that "Karma-52" was hit by enemy fire "is a very definite one."[9] But in April-May 1986, Fernando and Paul were widely believed to have simply flown into the water. General Donnelly may have shared that view and thus been reluctant to reward the "erring" crew with the nation's third highest award for valor (after the Medal of Honor and the Air Force Cross). That happenstance also had the benefit of deflecting any criticism of the decision to send nine jets across the downtown Tripoli target of Azziziyah Barracks. Of course, we now have strong reason to believe that the "pilot error" theory for the loss of "Karma-52" was incorrect.

It should also be noted that Fernando Ribas-Dominicci and Paul Lorence were not the only El Dorado Canyon flyers impacted by the USAFE stance on awards: one of the three lieutenant colonels who played a leadership role throughout the contingency and who flew as an element leader on the raid was denied a Distinguished Flying Cross for his efforts. Instead, he received only an Air Medal just like the rest of the line crewmen who flew the mission. It appears that the discriminator used to downgrade his contribution was the fact that he did not put his bombs on his assigned target. The fact that he could not bomb because of a systems failure and that he correctly held his fire and jettisoned his bombs at sea appears to have been ignored in deciding on his award.

As this chapter is written and all the unclassified facts become public, there are many of us who were involved in Operation El Dorado Canyon who continue to hope that appropriate recognition for the crew that perished is not a dead issue. Official reconsideration of the decisions made in 1986 regarding Silver Stars for Paul and Fernando remains our goal. Without exception, the crewmen who flew to Tripoli that night eagerly await that event.

There is a final footnote to this chapter. Among those who led the wing during this period, only Sam Westbrook and Cliff Bingham received the prestigious Legion of Merit medal for their performance at Lakenheath. Colonel Westbrook received his as he departed Lakenheath and assumed his new rank of brigadier general. Colonel Bingham, whose maintenance complex had been in the running for the best in USAFE, was initially awarded only a Meritorious Service Medal (MSM). Over two years later, after further justification had been submitted by Sam Westbrook, Cliff finally got his well-deserved Legion of Merit. The other colonels, including the author, received only the more common MSM. As mentioned earlier, there were 23,443 MSMs awarded by the Air Force in 1986. I attempted to officially decline the award but was informed after my retirement that I could not take that action. Instead, it was officially suggested that I might choose not to wear this MSM. I so choose.

# SUCCESS OR FAILURE

W as Operation El Dorado Canyon a success or a failure? In assessing the raid's effects, both the military and the political results of the mission must be examined. These factors are seldom unrelated. In the case of a combat mission meant to punish and deter terrorism, they are obviously closely intertwined. This discussion will begin with the easier, more objective assessment of the operation's military results.

The Operation El Dorado Canyon bombers took off from RAF Lakenheath with the objective of delivering seventy-two 500-pound, air-retarded bombs and forty-eight 2,000-pound Laser Guided Bombs on three target complexes in and around Tripoli. One obvious measure of the raid's success, therefore, is the number of those bombs that impacted on or very near their aiming points: the DMPIs mentioned earlier. By this standard, the one the participating crews judged themselves against in the first hours after landing, the mission was not a roaring success. Approximately one-third of the bombs were not delivered at all; a variety of F-111F system failures combined with stringent Rules Of Engagement resulted in several of the F-111Fs being forced to abort their attacks in the target area. As reported in several other sources, slightly relaxed ROE would have allowed some of these attacks to be prosecuted rather than being terminated.

Those who set the lofty standards for the raid, including Secretary of Defense Caspar Weinberger, have admitted that the rigid rules demanding fully operational weapons delivery systems played a major role in the mission's limited success in putting bombs on targets. [1]

An unclassified summary of the El Dorado Canyon bombing published in 1989 in the aviation book *F-111 Aardvark* revealed that four of the eleven aircraft that actually dropped bombs had hits on or very near their targets. [2] Of course, that equals only about twenty percent of the total weapons intended for the targets. But, of the LGBs dropped, roughly one-third found their targets. These figures do not seem representative of what the Air Force advertises as "precision bombing," so perhaps it is necessary to give the reader some historical perspective.

While measuring bombing accuracy is an inexact science with large margins for error, it has been attempted to some degree after every instance of aerial warfare. These studies reveal that the accuracy of bombing has been on a steady but slow increase ever since the birth of military aviation. The wildly inaccurate bombing of World War I was eclipsed by the results of World War II. The post-war Strategic Bombing Survey documented overall accuracies of approximately five percent—a quantum improvement over the first war. The combined numbers for the Korean and Vietnam wars would probably reveal improvement all the way to the ten-to-fifteen-percent range; the introduction of small numbers of practical guided bombs in Southeast Asia (WW II and Korean War developments were not very successful in this regard) would contribute to these lofty numbers.

As indicated earlier, for all the bombs actually dropped at Tripoli, El Dorado Canyon showed accuracies well above the historical averages. The figure is over thirty percent if only precision munitions, the Laser Guided Bombs, are counted. These figures are in line with the increased accuracy trend that has since been confirmed by Operation Desert Storm. Indeed, preliminary analysis of Desert Storm results point to accuracies for LGBs in the seventy-to-eighty-percent range. As that war went on, even higher hit rates were achieved with these weapons in what became a benign environment for the bombing aircraft. In the twelve minutes of combat that constituted Operation El Dorado Canyon, the environment was anything but benign.

But, as indicated above, the Libyan defenses did not play the major role in preventing aircraft from reaching their targets. Two attackers aborted well before reaching Tripoli; four others aborted due to system failures and ROE in or very near the target area; and only one of eighteen planes was shot down before it could drop its bombs. That left eleven jets which actually dropped, and only one of these eleven made a mistake which caused significant collateral damage. Their orders had called for them to inflict maximum visible damage while minimizing collateral damage, and the ROE that they had to follow was crystal clear as to which systems had to be working properly before bombs could be released. If the defenses are given credit for partially causing the errant bombs that struck near the French embassy, my tally of the overall attack on Tripoli looks like this:

| | | |
|---|---|---|
| **A.** | Hit Target | 4 of 18 |
| **B.** | Missed Target due to Defenses | 2 of 18 |
| **C.** | Missed Target for Unknown Reasons | 6 of 18 |
| **D.** | Aborted due to plane/ROE before Tripoli | 2 of 18 |
| **E.** | Aborted in target area due to plane/ROE | 4 of 18 |

Category C cannot be explained in any great detail in an unclassified volume, but it should be obvious to the reader that several of the problems outlined elsewhere in these pages contributed to those near misses. An example would be the problem with the coordinates of the Mediterranean island used to update the attackers' navigation systems. In the cockpits where this problem was not immediately evident, a significant error was introduced into the computerized bombing systems which later interfered with the final bombing runs. This and other minor problems played a role in the six missed attacks which are listed in the "unknown" category above.

The reader may ask whether or not the Libyan defenses were a big part of the unknown reasons for category C's misses. While I do not discount their playing some part, I reject the theory that those defenses were a dominant factor. That stance seemed popular immediately after the raid, especially among the military and political leaders who had to explain what had happened. Invariably, they seemed to fall back on the easiest and most obvious explanation for every problem in aviation; crew error. In secretary Weinberger's book *Fighting for Peace* he emphasizes the youth of the aircrews in explaining the unfortunate collateral damage. The implication that inexperience under fire was a major factor is barely hidden between the lines. In David Martin's *Best Laid Plans*, Major General Forgan is quoted as saying that, "there's no way to estimate the effect of hostile fire on pilots." Admiral Kelso adds that at night, "every SAM looks like it's coming at you. . . . Most of these kids had never seen a SAM fired in anger."

The secretary, the general, and the admiral were all correct in their general observations about combat and its effects, but unfortunately their statements can be interpreted as implying that aircrew error was the main reason for the raid's problems. The monumental length of the mission, the known fragility of the F-111 and some of its critical subsystems, and the complications of the night attack were not given adequate weight. More importantly, the last-minute major changes that tripled the size of the mission and caused the final hectic hours before takeoff were totally disregarded as possible causes for the raid's problems. In military aviation, errors and misjudgements at almost all levels can be overcome by the men with the control sticks in their hands—if they are flexible, competent, and very lucky. If however they are somehow unable to fix it all, they often serve as whipping boys for the criticism that rightfully ought to be directed elsewhere.

All this is not to say that the raid was not a military success. In fact, the national leadership, including President Reagan and many of the leaders cited above, was effusive in its praise of the mission's accomplishments. The president declared victory and simultaneously cautioned against euphoria the day after the raid when he noted that the U.S. had "won but a single engagement in a long battle against terrorism."[3] That same day, Pentagon spokesman Robert Sims acknowledged the "extremely difficult circumstances" of the raid, and speculated that nothing like this mission had occurred "in the U.S. military annals."[4] Mr. Sims then went on to say that all five of the mission's targets at both Benghazi and Tripoli had been struck effectively in a "flawless professional performance." The evidence for this claim was clear in the case of the 48th Wing's attacks on Tripoli: videotapes from three separate cockpits confirmed that all three targets had been hit. Secretary Weinberger's book, written four years after the mission, details the damage to each of the targets which he first saw on those videos, and rightly suggests that they were "the most dramatic evidence of our success."[5]

Successful bombing of three "first-look" (never before seen other than in photos) targets at night was a significant achievement in itself. To do it in the teeth of strong, alerted defenses after a six-plus-hour flight was just short of incredible. An indication of just how significant this accomplishment was came in a training exercise conducted at the base I retired from after El Dorado Canyon. A wing equipped with the same night all-weather Pave Tack attack system deployed to Eglin AFB, Florida, in 1987 to test their ability to strike "first-look" targets under simulated combat conditions. They flew their sorties during daylight and with no one shooting at them. Their two-week evaluation ended with the following score: eight attempts, zero hits.

Militarily, the Statue of Liberty Wing had done itself proud. There was no reason then and there is no reason now for anyone who flew the mission to feel downhearted about the overall results. Should more of the bombs carried towards Libya that night have been delivered accurately to their targets? The answer is an almost certain yes. Were the major factors that prevented that from happening within the control of those who occupied the darkened Aardvark cockpits? The answer is a resounding no. General Donnelly was right, as quoted by David Martin, when he said that, "we didn't hit it as well as we wanted."[6] That feeling was shared by every crewman and every colonel at Lakenheath as soon as the raid's checkered bombing results were known. But I believe the general and others were off the mark when they may have seized on the aircrews as the best excuse for what had happened. Based on the evidence spelled out in these pages, I submit that those skilled crews were the primary reason that the mission enjoyed *any* military success whatsoever. As an anonymous contributor to Andrew Cockburn's *Playboy* article suggested, "They didn't do too badly considering what they were up against."[7] That comment is a tremendous understatement.

In summary, it might be said that the attack on Tripoli was a conditional, or "asterisked," military success. The interservice joint planning and execution of the mission was, on the whole, a notable success story that will eventually be told in detail elsewhere. The performance of the "smart weapons" used on some targets was also a noteworthy achievement; it translated into additional procurement and political support for same, and served as a precursor of the unparalleled destruction they would unleash during 1991's Desert Storm. However, there is no one, including the author, who can claim that the Navy and Air Force fully met their pre-raid objectives, except to the extent that some visible damage was achieved at each of the five target complexes engaged. In a brief perspective which suggested that "precision bombing" is an oxymoron, the *American Defense Annual* of 1987–1988 nevertheless admitted that, "The raid against Tripoli was a clear military success, if not quite a textbook operation." However, recalling that the operation was as much a political act as it was military, the next question must be, How effective was the raid politically?

Immediately after the mission, there was some significant doubt that it could be considered anything but a political disaster. Various pundits speculated on the major damage which had been done to the NATO alliance; to our relations with the Arab world; and to U.S. bilateral relations with Italy, France, Spain, and England among others. A wave of revenge terrorist attacks was predicted, not only against U.S. bases and interests overseas, but also in the streets and neighborhoods of Hometown, U.S.A. If this had been a combat mission in the war against terrorism, was it not likely that it would cause counterattacks contributing to a "spiral of violence" that would see American blood flowing in many unpredictable places? These concerns found voice in the newspapers of the world, and were accompanied by cautions that subsequent raids against Libya or other nations sponsoring terrorism might be even less popular and more counterproductive. Among those stating such views were eminent national security experts Robert McFarlane, Zbigniew Brzezinski, and Brent Scowcroft. There were many who agreed with Mr. Brzezinski's quoted view that, "we haven't really dealt a blow to terrorism; we've just made ourselves feel good."[8]

While the efficacy of the "Feel-Good Libya Raid" was doubted by some within the U.S., many Americans were squarely behind the effort. Most seemed to share the feeling that a turning point had been reached in the battle against state-sponsored terrorism. They agreed with the assessment of one expert on terrorism, H.E. Meyer, who celebrated the fact that "At last the victims of terrorism are shooting back."[9] Despite the statistical odds, millions of us had come to feel that we were becoming ever more popular targets; the raid provided some much needed relief from that perception of helplessness. The *Providence Journal* called the military action "precise, proportionate and timely."[10] Perhaps the best one-line summary of American thought in the immediate wake of the raid was encompassed in the headline that accompanied Bill Shipp's editorial in the *Atlanta Constitution* of April 18: "Three Cheers for the President's Decision to Attack Libya—I Think."

The widespread, almost unconditional support in the United States was in marked contrast to the reaction in Europe. The attack on Libya was widely rejected by Europeans as a useful tool against terrorism. Pointing to the EEC's agreement on antiterrorist political and economic sanctions, reached belatedly on the morning of April 14, many Europeans suggested that the U.S. had overstepped itself in a simplistic, Rambo-like approach to the complex problem of terrorism. That criticism failed to acknowledge the role that imminent U.S. military action had played in forcing any concerted European steps against Colonel Qaddafi. The minimal actions of April 14 were reinforced immediately after the raid, with expulsions of Libyan envoys across the continent, formal condemnations of Libya's role in sponsoring terrorism, and various other political and economic actions adding muscle to what had been a weak European non-policy toward Qaddafi's Libya. The *New York Times* speculated in "The Bombs Bestir the Allies," the aptly titled April 24 editorial: "Does anyone doubt that if achieved a year ago, such allied solidarity could have saved lives, including innocent Libyan lives?"

Those innocent lives were the primary focus of European recriminations against President Reagan and the raid. With a healthy boost from Libya's propaganda machine, most such criticism described Operation El Dorado Canyon as unjustified or illegal, and recommended further negotiation through the United Nations to bring Qaddafi to bay. The killing of thirty-seven Libyans and wounding of over ninety others provided ammunition for the many Europeans who now saw themselves as even bigger targets in an expanding war with terrorists.[11] In that war, it was argued, Libya had now gained the support of the whole Arab, African, and non-aligned world. The assumption of that support and its implications for the future seemed to be borne out by the brief wave of terrorist revenge actions taken in the days following the mission. Mentioned earlier in these pages, those attacks helped explain why over eighty percent of the suddenly exposed British said that they expected Libyan terrorism to increase after the raid. In Rome, the Italians voiced similar sentiments as they reacted to Libya's abortive missile attack against Lampedusa Island within hours of the bombing. In Paris, irritation with the U.S. independent action was balanced to an extent by the growing realization that many French citizens had been outraged that the task force had been denied clearance through French airspace—apparently average French people were more fed up with terrorism than was the French government.

The general European disdain for the attack against terrorism did not find much understanding on this side of the Atlantic. The French found themselves the objects of widespread derision and insulting jokes on the Johnny Carson show. The word "allies" appeared in quotes in several editorials questioning the behavior and motivation of our "supposed friends." The fact that U.S. personnel serving in NATO in defense of Europe had died in terrorist attacks caused Americans to wonder what sort of allies we had been protecting for forty years. And the indisputable ineffectiveness of doing nothing against terrorism—attacks worldwide had increased by over sixty percent between 1983 and 1985—made Americans wonder why Europe in general now favored only economic and diplomatic options. The reactions in the U.S. were often barely restrained. An editorialist for the *Atlanta Journal* insisted that "What we must feel in response [to European timidity] is anger, pity, and contempt."[12]

However, when emotions cooled within weeks of the raid, calmer voices were heard on both sides of the Atlantic. On April 20, the *London Sunday Times* pointed out that, while the U.S.

had no right to unquestioning obedience from its allies, it "had every right to expect better of [the] European allies last week," especially since those Europeans "offered no credible alternative policy." That same day, an editorial in the *St. Louis Globe-Democrat* suggested that the U.S. raid might be the beginning of the end for Libyan terrorism.[13] That overly optimistic attitude was at least partly based on one phenomenon that had been observed after the mission: the Soviet Union had shown no inclination to come to Colonel Qaddafi's aid before, during, or even after the attack. Indeed, the Russians' reaction was just the first of several unpredictable events that resulted from El Dorado Canyon.

There was some loud posturing on the part of the Soviet Union after the raid, including accusations that the bombing was a "criminal action." But despite those public outcries, the Russians took no major action to reassure Colonel Qaddafi concerning their intentions, or lack of same, to defend his country. His subsequent plea to enter the Warsaw Pact was largely ignored by the Soviets and the other pact nations. The cold shoulder he received from the Russians was the first of many Qaddafi would experience after the bombing. Instead of widespread, unquestioning support, the Arab world provided only minimal public expressions of sympathy; and even those statements were balanced by reported private assurances of understanding for the U.S. stance. Neither did the Third world seem to respond too vigorously to Colonel Qaddafi's cries for solidarity. All in all, the new coalition against the West and the U.S. that many assumed would form in the wake of the bombing never took shape. Instead, Qaddafi's Libya found itself abandoned and isolated. This turn of events was described in detail in reports that developed within six months of the attack. They disclosed the mental state of Qaddafi, the status of his changed political power within Libya, and a growing consensus that the mission had been a resounding political success.[14]

During the period two to six months after the raid, observers noted a dramatic change in the statements and actions emanating from Tripoli. Reports of Qaddafi's weakening at home included comments on his country's diplomatic isolation, the Soviets' "arm's length" treatment of their erratic ally, and the virtual absence of terrorist activity attributable to Libya. The *Christian Sci-*

*ence Monitor* of June 25 reported that "terrorist attacks sponsored by Tripoli have all but ceased." That development and the subdued, secluded life of Colonel Qaddafi were also remarked upon in the *Hartford Courant* two days later.

The latter aspect of Qaddafi's life in Tripoli had been in evidence as soon as the bombs stopped falling on April 15. Colonel Qaddafi had been seen only fleetingly in the weeks afterward, and even then only in controlled situations. He canceled public appearances and, to all intents and purposes, seemed to vanish into the desert for days at a time. According to some observers who saw him after the mission, he had seemed extremely quiet, distracted, and even "unhinged." No western reporter was granted an interview until over two months had passed. The most likely explanation for this, as reported by at least one source (the *Dallas Morning News*), was that he had been asleep in his tent on the night of April 14–15, 1986.[15] The good news for the colonel was that the tent had not been targeted; the bad news was that 2,000-pound bombs made tremendous noise and had crushing concussive effect when they impacted within a few hundred feet of him. The collapse of his tent around him undoubtedly contributed to Colonel Qaddafi's behavior in the following months.

The tent's partial destruction was just one of many pieces of evidence that lent credence to the theory that the mission's real target had been Colonel Qaddafi himself. The controversial decision to send nine jets against Azziziyah was another. Within hours of the raid, rumors began to spread that those in power in Washington had not-so-subtly made every effort to ensure that the Libyan leader would not survive El Dorado Canyon. Off-the-cuff remarks from highly placed sources that they would not have been disturbed by Qaddafi's death seemed to seal the bargain. The post-mission rumors and theories finally culminated in a lengthy article by Seymour M. Hersh in the February 22, 1987, issue of the *New York Times Magazine*. With the self-explanatory title of "Target Qaddafi," the piece strove mightily to support the premise that the real target had indeed been Muammar Qaddafi. But the article was flawed in that it reached beyond the circumstantial evidence it presented to an erroneous conclusion. That conclusion was that the nine F-111Fs targeted against the Azziziyah Barracks complex were really after Colonel Qaddafi and his family. Had the author known the specific aiming points of those nine aircraft, he would have realized the weakness of his argument. Only two of the nine Aardvarks were assigned to the headquarters building, which was known to sometimes serve as quarters for Qaddafi and his family. However, no one was certain of his or their location on the night of the raid. In the final intelligence briefings, the 48th's crews were specifically told that Colonel Qaddafi's whereabouts were unknown. Based on that uncertainty, an assassination attempt would have necessarily included Colonel Qaddafi's tent as a prime target. As stated above and in Chapter Six, the colonel's tent, his most commonly used sleeping quarters, was never targeted.

That single piece of evidence, in the author's opinion, destroys the theory that Operation El Dorado Canyon was an assassination attempt. To mount a huge aerial task force, fly it over 2,500 miles, and then not bomb the most likely location of the supposed "target" does not make any military sense. Those of us who were on the scene at Lakenheath do not believe that Muammar Qaddafi was our target. It appears to have been a matter of chance that he was anywhere near where the bombs fell. It is possible, of course, that history will prove us wrong: prove that the raid was a machination of the Ollie North–led "Iran-Contra" gang, and that the 48th Wing was their unwitting tool. In that event, history will also record that the tent should have been targeted if that was the mission's goal.

All this is not to say that Colonel Qaddafi's demise may not have been desired by those who ordered the raid. (If avoiding his death had been a goal, there were more than enough targets among the thirty-plus we had planned for which would have served to display visible damage without necessarily endangering him or his family.) If his death was a secret objective of someone in Washington, it must have been hoped that it would occur as a seeming byproduct of the mission. The crews at Lakenheath had been aware of the possibility even as they sat through their final briefings; the assignment of nine attackers to Qaddafi's headquarters raised eyebrows despite the fact that the tent was not an aim point. If the raid *was* an assassination attempt, it was a subtle one that apparently took into account the legal prohibitions against such action. And it was never revealed to those flying the jets.

By July 1986, the cautious assessments of conditional success began to give way to outright declarations of victory. "Bombing Gadhafi [sic] Worked," wrote David Ignatius in the *Washington Post* of July 13.[16] His points, in turn, were that the mission had not bolstered Qaddafi at home, it had not strengthened his relations with the Russians, it had not forced the Arab world to rally to him, and it had not destroyed U.S. relations with Europe. Most importantly, Operation El Dorado Canyon had exploded the myth of Libya as intimidating and exposed the colonel as "weak, isolated, and vulnerable." While Libyan terrorism had not halted, it had certainly been curbed. A U.S. official was quoted as saying that the whole of Qaddafi's "terror apparatus seems to be in disarray." Of course, whatever disarray had occurred was not a direct result of the bombing, but an indirect result of the concerted western economic and political actions the raid had prompted.

The reduced sponsorship of terrorism by Libya was confirmed by an Israeli study published in August 1986. That study gave optimistic assessments of the mission's effects on both worldwide terrorism and on Libya-sponsored terrorism. Unfortunately, only the latter has been in decline in the five-plus years that have passed. As reported in the May 1989 *Department of State Bulletin*, Libya was deemed responsible for nineteen terrorist attacks in 1986, but had only directed six attacks each year in 1987 and 1988. Other nations thought to sponsor terrorism, and considered to be possible targets for similar retaliation, showed similar trends. The numbers for Syria, for instance, were thirty-four attacks in 1985; six in 1986; one in 1987; and none in 1988. In 1987, Syria went so far in its efforts to lower its pro-terrorism profile that it expelled the Abu Nidal organization (it is now reported to be based partly in Libya and partly in Iraq). Nevertheless, overall terrorist activity worldwide continued to rise—records were set for total numbers of attacks in both 1987 and 1988—until 1989. In May 1991, the U.S. State Department reported that a thirty-eight percent drop in terrorist attacks from 1988 to 1989 had been followed by a further fifteen percent drop in terrorism from 1989 to 1990.[17] In addition, 1990 passed without a major terrorism spectacular. The war on international state-sponsored terrorism continues, and the good guys appear to be gaining the upper hand.

Other evidence seems to support that conclusion. The 1985
*Reader's Guide to Periodical Literature* provides over two and a
half pages of references to terrorists and terrorism. The 1989 version has less than one and a half pages. While Libya figured
prominently on those pages in 1985 and 1986, there are no references at all to Libya in the "terrorism" category for 1988 or 1989.
But for those of us who lived in Europe during the mid-1980's,
the real payoff of the attack on Libya came in the somewhat
subjective assessment that Americans were no longer such promi-
nent, desirable terrorist targets. The headlines in the years since
the attack, with one major exception—the bombing of Pan Am
Flight 103—have been remarkably free of blown up U.S. airlin-
ers and widely and repeatedly targeted Americans. Of course, terrorism has not stopped; in certain specific countries and
situations, it remains as dangerous a threat as ever. But the cyni-
cal, brazen targeting of American citizens by countries who formerly felt themselves invulnerable has all but ceased. The men
and women of the 48th "Statue of Liberty" Wing can take pride
in the small role they played in that accomplishment.

As David Ignatius suggested five years ago, "Bombing Libya
was an ugly act . . . but it achieved a useful purpose if . . . it
began to change the political balance in the Middle East away
from radicalism and toward moderation."[18] That is what seems
to have happened, beginning right after the raid when Qaddafi
realized his vulnerability to both external and internal forces. By
August of that year, Libyans were reported to be openly questioning the colonel's leadership for the first time. The average
Libyan apparently did not mind spending the state's wealth on
arms so long as the only western response was threats. Attacks by
armed military aircraft were an entirely different story. Qaddafi's
newfound moderation has appeared to continue in the face of a
moribund Libyan economy and the ongoing restiveness of his
followers. By late 1988, the post-raid Libyan enmity toward the
U.S. was being softened as Colonel Qaddafi and his government
made an effort to connect that animosity to the outgoing president and his administration. Only then Vice President Bush was
spared: in an article titled "Libya, Despite Animus, Looks Toward U.S. Ties," the *Washington Post* reported that the colonel
favored Bush in the November election since, "he has learned a
lot from [President] Reagan's mistakes."

One year later, Colonel Qaddafi was dealing with President Bush and the new administration in a "decidedly restrained" manner. A *Washington Post* article on September 2, 1989, noted his subdued manner and described him as "ever hopeful of better relations with the United States." The same report noted Qaddafi's twentieth anniversary in power, and described the dispatch of Italy's Foreign Minister Gianni de Michelis to Tripoli as "the highest-ranking Western official to visit Libya in five years." Libya and its mercurial leader seemed to be exhibiting the traits of a nation trying, at least to an extent, to rejoin the congenial ranks of what we, in our more sanguine moments, like to call the "Family of Nations." As this book is written, those newly discovered Libyan characteristics of moderation and restraint seem to be continuing—to a degree. Colonel Qaddafi's recent revelation in a television interview that he would have attacked New York and Washington, D.C., with long-range missiles in 1986 if he had possessed them, seems to be a throwback to an earlier, more radical time.

It is unrealistic to expect Libya's status in the world community to change markedly while Colonel Qaddafi makes such statements. There is one public declaration, however, that could conceivably help Libya improve its international standing. A declaration by Colonel Qaddafi himself, stating that no retaliatory action will ever be taken against the men who, in performing their military duties, bombed Tripoli in 1986, might have some positive effect. It is difficult to imagine the circumstances that would allow such action, but I wish that it would happen. Nevertheless, even if such an "amnesty" was declared, its effects would be a matter of speculation and of our assessment of Qaddafi's sincerity—in the real world, the El Dorado Canyon crewmen would be unlikely to take such a statement on faith.

Col. Muammar Qaddafi's sincerity remains highly suspect primarily in reference to the one truly horrendous act of anti-American terrorism that has been perpetrated since Operation El Dorado Canyon. In December 1988, the ghastly murder of 270 people aboard Pan Am Flight 103 and on the ground at Lockerbie, Scotland, shocked the world and began an intensive search for those responsible. It is painful for anyone who had anything to do with the 1986 raid to acknowledge that this heinous terrorist attack may have been made in revenge for the bombing of Tripoli and Benghazi.

From the beginning, there has been speculation that Libya might have sponsored the assault. While the author's research into this matter has been limited, two facts stand out clearly in the body of periodical literature that has reported on the subject. First, Shiite Iran seems to have had a more significant reason for sponsoring a revenge attack against a U.S. airliner: the July 3, 1988, shootdown of Iran Air Flight 655 by the U.S. Navy. That sad series of errors, known collectively as "The Vincennes Incident," was the rationale cited by at least one terrorist group in its claim of responsibility immediately afterward. As a result, there has been some intermittent consensus that Iran was far more likely to have been the sponsor of the Lockerbie tragedy. Second, the passage of time after El Dorado Canyon and the failure of Libya or any of its terrorist guests to claim credit for the attack has seemed to argue against assigning blame to Colonel Qaddafi. Nevertheless, it is certainly premature to absolve Libya. As the summer of 1991 began, new reports surfaced linking Libya to the destruction of Pan Am Flight 103 through several pieces of circumstantial evidence discovered during continuing French and British investigations.[19]

If these new reports prove true and are corroborated, the policy precedent set by President Reagan will face a significant test. The most important question may be whether there is any ad hoc statute of limitations on retaliation. Other critical questions will also require answers. Among them: what is a proportionate response to the downing of Pam Am Flight 103? Should any retaliation be tempered due to the fact that it took several years to identify the murderers and their sponsors? If so, what new precedent is being set? Can the nations fighting against terrorism accept that precedent?

Those questions will require answers when and if the facts concerning Libya, Qaddafi, and Pan Am Flight 103 prove to be as incontrovertible as was the evidence in 1986. However, at this writing, there is also a body of conflicting information that points to other countries and terrorist groups as possible sources for the Lockerbie bomb. In the absence of substantive proof, we may never be in a position to take firm action against those we suspect of destroying Pan Am Flight 103 and murdering 270 innocent people. The various ongoing investigations may end without authoritatively determining guilt. In that event, no one other than the terrorists who performed the act may ever know the truth.

Even with the cloud of Pan Am Flight 103 hanging over the subject, the majority of writers and reporters who have examined the issue seem to share this author's view that Operation El Dorado Canyon was a significant political success. As *Air Force Magazine* noted in September 1986, "The Libya raid demonstrated the long reach and telling impact of modern airpower properly employed." More importantly, the attack also demonstrated bilateral cooperation within the NATO alliance that permitted that firepower display. This factor undoubtedly had a telling effect on Libya and other nations that sponsor terrorism.

The involvement of Great Britain, although minimal militarily, was a huge factor in the raid's political success. It helped to counter the image of the United States as a trigger-happy cowboy on the international scene. It also showed unpredictable terrorist nations that the West might not always be predictable in its responses to their actions—after all, if Mrs. Thatcher said yes this time, might not Turkey or France go along if required in the future? Perhaps it is not an understatement to suggest that the raid on Libya would not have taken place in any form without the cooperation of at least one ally. Since the post-Falklands British were the most likely to provide assistance, their cooperation, in the author's view, was the driving factor which dictated that F-111s based in the U.K. be used to bomb Tripoli. There was no other telling military argument to justify this choice.

The official position, stated repeatedly after the raid, was that the five selected targets dictated the use of Aardvarks from England—the carriers *America* and *Coral Sea* could not service all of them by themselves.[20] That argument seems simplistic in that there was nothing magic about the number five or the specific targets selected. The number and location of the targets was not critical to the decision to send the 48th on this mission: I suggest that the presence of ten carriers in the Mediterranean might have resulted in the selection of fifteen, or perhaps twenty, targets—enough so that the Navy would have been unable to do the job without Air Force help. Why would the number of targets be arbitrarily adjusted to force that action? One suggestion is that interservice politics played a role: the Air Force lobbied for a part of the mission. The *Wall Street Journal* of April 21, 1986, made that claim, adding that General Rogers, the Army general commanding all U.S. forces in Europe, had selected the five targets to display the force projection capabilities of our land-based forces. While I doubt the validity of this claim, even if it has any basis in fact, General Rogers should be congratulated for his political acumen. He forced the minimal involvement of a single, somewhat reluctant ally, and made Operation El Dorado Canyon a singular success.

I believe it is much more likely that President Reagan and his inner circle understood the necessity of involving one or more of our allies. It was crucial that the United States not act unilaterally. Because we did not, the beneficial political effects of the raid were multiplied. The cooperation of the British and the lack of same from the French and Spanish set the stage for the granddaddy of all fighter missions. The F-111F crews of the 48th who flew it played a major role in that international drama, and the positive repercussions of their actions continue to be seen today.

# COMBAT AND COSMETICS

The United States Air Force, like all modern enter-
prises, attempts to measure its capabilities through
objective, quantifiable criteria. In the case of combat
units like the 48th Wing, those criteria include factors which
must be obvious to almost anyone. Numbers of flyable aircraft,
trained crews, and available bombs and bullets are among the
things considered when a fighter wing reports its Combat ("C")
status. A wing commander's job largely consists of ensuring that
the wing meets the benchmarks established for these variables at
all times, while striving to maintain the highest possible state of
readiness. The wing's status is transmitted daily to higher headquarters where flag officers up to and including the Air Force
chief of staff monitor the overall warfighting ability of the service.

On April 16, 1986, the report for the 48th TFW undoubtedly
showed a unit less capable of combat than many of its sister
wings. A superb crew and their aircraft had been lost, and the
returning aircraft and exhausted crews were not immediately
ready to return to combat. In addition, the wing's stock of ordnance had been momentarily depleted. All in all, by the objective, quantifiable measures used to gauge combat capability, the
Statue of Liberty Wing was probably in the lower half of U.S.
Air Force fighter wings reporting that day.

But, as the history of military endeavor has repeatedly proven, combat capability consists of more than the external, countable features of a military organization. There are several intangibles which, though difficult to measure, are thought to be among the essentials that contribute to a military organization's effectiveness. They include esprit de corps, leadership, cohesiveness, and courage. If these intangibles are taken into account, the 48th Wing was *the* most capable fighting unit in the Air Force on April 16, 1986.

It is difficult to overstate just how high morale was at the time, but it is safe to say that the F-111 inferiority complex I have previously explained all but disappeared in the wake of the mission. Our transient ramp, where visiting jets from other wings park each weekend, became crowded with many types of aircraft which we had not previously seen. The officers' club became the scene of many informal briefings for visiting fighter pilots on what had *really* happened over Libya. The 48th was combat-tested and combat-ready to an extent unmatched anywhere else in the Air Force. Unfortunately, that status proved to be short-lived. Within eighteen months of the raid, the intangible strengths that made the 48th TFW so combat-capable in April of 1986 had been significantly diminished.

In May, the new wing commander began his reign as "Wing King," having apparently been given a clear charter by his superiors. What was needed were changes in the appearance of RAF Lakenheath; a new and improved base would provide a better home for the proud units it hosted. This shift back to peacetime priorities, from combat to cosmetics, had a predictable effect over time: the wing's unique combat capability was gradually eroded. Actually, eroded is the wrong word; it disappeared under multiple coats of tan paint with pinstripes.

The appearance of a military base is not unimportant. It often sets the tone for the entire organization and for the individuals within it. It is also considered to be the initial visible evidence of the state of discipline and morale within the unit. It can be all of these things—and a lot less.

When Gen. Wilbur C. Creech took command of the Air Force's Tactical Air Command in 1978, he grabbed the reins of an underfunded organization which showed signs of neglect in certain areas. Despite leadership that had planted the seeds for realistic training through intense exercises like "Red Flag," TAC displayed visible evidence of deterioration, to include dismal statistics on the command's flying activities (low numbers of sorties; high accident rates; etc.) and poor physical working conditions for the command's people, especially its maintenance personnel. General Creech attacked those and other problems with great success; I will not detail his achievements here, but refer the reader to Tom Peters's books on excellence for additional information—the general's long tenure and many successes at TAC are used by Mr. Peters as a case study in leadership in the pursuit of excellence. The foundation for General Creech's successes, however, bears closer examination.

General Creech was a firm believer in improving the physical image of an individual or organization in order to enhance performance. His background as a leader of the Air Force's primary image builders, the Thunderbirds, was evident in his stated philosophy paraphrased here: an excellent organization always offers an excellent appearance. Unfortunately, that rule has a corollary—not every organization that looks good is good. Without taking this into account, General Creech's emphasis on the cosmetic aspects of military performance produced a major air command that was much better than the one he inherited, but not as good as it looked. Fueled by the funding windfalls of the early Reagan years, each TAC base was transformed into something of a showplace. Inevitably, the general's philosophy of excellence spread as his protégés advanced, reaching Europe in full force under General Donnelly. With it came buckets of TAC-style paint; if it worked in the States, surely it could work in Europe.

But paint was not the only visible evidence of this new attitude. Witness the many "people programs," such as the Mildenhall officers' club. These initiatives resulted in some controversial efforts to enhance base appearance and to improve morale. One such program was the "Avenue of Flags."

What could be better for morale at each base in Europe than an avenue of flags displaying the banners of all fifty states? It would remind everyone of our roots and homes, while sprucing up each base with a colorful display area. If your analysis of the idea stops there, you are likely to have favored the flags. But, if you took into account the shortage of real estate at most U.S.

bases in Europe, as well as costs, the idea lost its appeal. The end result was that each new avenue of flags established in USAFE prompted a rash of complaints—hardly an indicator of improved morale. Fortunately, at Lakenheath this particular problem did not affect us—either British law or the Status of Forces Agreement with the United Kingdom permitted the display of only three flags (the Royal ensign; the RAF ensign; and the Stars and Stripes) at U.S. bases in the U.K.

The 48th did not escape the impact of other similar initiatives. In order to "build morale," we were directed to name our aircraft shelters after famous figures in aviation history. Today, it is my understanding that every HAS (Hardened Aircraft Shelter—another name for a TAB Vee) in Europe sports a sign with a military aviation hero's name emblazoned on it. The maintainers and the flyers are largely oblivious to them, but their superiors point them out to visiting VIPs and congressmen as evidence of the superb morale within their units.

But these initiatives were basically harmless. The costs were tiny (in defense budget terms); the actions taken did not degrade combat capability; and the overall impact was barely discernible. Only the cosmetic change itself stood out, but not to the extent that a base's mission was compromised. That remained true until the "TAC painting" initiatives began.

Painting a base in the United States is not very controversial. Since attacks on our stateside bases are not probable in the early days of some future war, it will not matter if a white base stands out against a desert background, or if a tan base is readily visible within the Louisiana bayou.

But, in Europe in 1986, painting a base had definite combat implications. Almost all NATO bases were within easy reach of Warsaw Pact fighter bombers. They were considered by experts on both sides of the Iron Curtain to be among the highest priority targets for those aircraft. Painting a base in Europe, therefore, could directly affect combat capability—some color schemes could make a base a visible beacon for attackers. Seeing a target from a distance—"early acquisition," in Air Force parlance—is very important to a successful attack. Late acquisition, on the other hand, can ruin many bomb runs: last-second adjustments must be made, bombs miss by a few more yards than they might, and the target is spared destruction. Accomplishing this is the goal of many "airbase survivability" initiatives the services have undertaken. Unsymmetrical color schemes, camouflage, and cheap aircraft decoys are a few of the actions taken to throw off the enemy's aim.[1] Individual wings have made other decisions to further improve their odds of surviving an air attack.

Which brings us back to RAF Lakenheath and the 48th Wing—in the months following the raid, on a base where combat capability had been the raison d'être, the wing undertook a major face-lifting program with tan paint and pinstripes as prime ingredients. Set in the unrelentingly green Suffolk countryside, all major buildings had their appearance enhanced by a color scheme favored at TAC headquarters in Virginia. During August 1986 alone, 110 buildings received a new coat of tan paint.[2]

Did the base need new paint? The answer is "almost certainly." But the men and women of the 48th who had recently executed the Air Force's only combat mission in over a decade had reason to question their service's priorities. Base appearance was important, but not to the extent that it impacted on combat capability. The turnaround in emphasis even extended to the sandbags stacked in various locations around the field to absorb bomb shrapnel. In one example of how cosmetics had overcome combat, all of the remaining sandbags at RAF Lakenheath were removed during the last hours prior to a visit of the new commander in chief of USAFE, apparently solely because they looked unattractive.[3] During my tour of duty there, I had heard criticisms of money going to "splinter protection" when so many "people programs" were short of funds. It occurred to me that if bombs ever began to fall, those behind the sandbags would probably think of them as our very best people program.

One result of the Statue of Liberty Wing's painting and renovation was a decline in morale. The actions taken spoke louder than any words used to justify them, with a resulting predictable drop in the fighting spirit of the unit. That trend continued until July 1987, when a new wing commander arrived. That officer was apparently able to restore much of what had been lost, and subsequently earned promotion to brigadier general—not being saddled with an onerous refurbishment program probably helped him in his efforts.

But, as this book goes to press, RAF Lakenheath remains painted mostly light tan with pinstripes, in sharp contrast to the green fields of East Anglia which surround it. The demise of the Warsaw Pact has reduced any sense of urgency regarding this issue, but in 1987 it was still a sore point with the El Dorado Canyon veterans. Colonel Barber discovered this first-hand one day as he returned to RAF Lakenheath on an F-111F training mission. Several miles from the base on final approach, his right-seater, an experienced WSO with a full-up combat orientation even though he had not flown to Tripoli a year earlier, listened as his wing commander commented on how nice the base looked. The WSO sincerely replied, "Yes Sir, it sure does; but it's a good thing we're not a Flogger."[4] "Flogger" is the NATO code name for a type of Soviet fighter bomber that could be among the first to reach England in the event of war. If that unlikely circumstance were to happen tomorrow, the Flogger crews would find a base that stands out in more ways than one. And unfortunately, due to its color scheme, they would almost certainly find the base.

In the wake of Operation Desert Storm and its unprecedented victory through airpower, it may seem ludicrous to focus on the Air Force's peacetime attitude toward combat. After all, the war against Iraq was won largely through the efforts of the allied air forces, with the United States Air Force providing the lion's share of the effort over both Iraq and Kuwait. There is no question that many post–Southeast Asia actions have been vindicated, including the establishment of realistic training like "Red Flag" and emphasis on sophisticated weapons and accuracy in their delivery. With such a historic victory as evidence, how can anyone question the service's full dedication to combat?

The answer, of course, is that there is every reason to believe that the U.S. Air Force could have improved on its superb performance of 1991. The improvement I refer to would not have required newer aircraft or better weapons. It could have been achieved entirely by the men and women of the service. The only requirement to have reached this enhanced level of performance would have been a deeper dedication and closer attention to peacetime actions that enhance the service's day-to-day combat capability. Included in that broad statement is the rejection of actions and options that inherently reduce combat capability. The U.S. Air Force of 1991 has obviously been successful in eliminating many of the factors that detract from its military performance. But those who love the service are always engaged in a never-ending campaign to minimize those factors.

While toasting the impressive achievements of U.S. airpower in Desert Storm, it is appropriate to call for an attitude that will make the Air Force's next combat outing even better. After all, the situational factors that made airpower so effective in the desert may be entirely lacking in some future combat. In those tougher circumstances, perhaps without time to train and acclimate, the peacetime mindset of the organization and of the individual commanders who lead it may prove the difference between success and failure. In that regard, it should be noted that one of the first major initiatives of the Air Force after Desert Storm has been to announce the development and testing of a new dress uniform.

One last footnote regarding Desert Storm is appropriate to this story. While the war's complete results will take some time to become public, conversations with Air Force personnel based worldwide have already revealed one of Desert Storm's best kept secrets: the twenty-year-old F-111Fs of the 48th Wing were among the operation's biggest stars! While most publicity was being lavished on cruise missiles, the Stealth Fighters, the Wild Weasels, the F-15Es, the A-10s, and the MiG-killing F-15Cs, the ancient Aardvark was piling up the most impressive Bomb Damage Assessments (BDA) of any of the coalition aircraft that took part in the unprecedented air campaign. Utilizing a mature weapons system—one with the bugs worked out of it—the Statue of Liberty Wing F-111F crews were the primary deliverers of the LGBs that devastated Saddam Hussein's airbases, infrastructure, and tank forces, roughly in that order. While the official statistics upon which this claim is made are likely to take months to see the light of day, there was a public revelation near the end of

Desert Storm that seems to confirm it. The reported cumulative total of Iraqi tanks destroyed stood at 1,950 on the same day that an article about the 48th Wing credited the unit with 750 tank kills. Using those numbers, my math suggests that, at that point in the conflict, a single wing with less than 70 aircraft (out of nearly 2,000 allied planes) had accomplished almost forty percent of all Iraqi armor kills. Another knowledgeable source who was in Saudi Arabia throughout the war has suggested that the final figures will place the F-111Fs' totals closer to fifty percent. An *Air Force Times* article in May 1991 credited the wing with destroying 920 tanks, 245 hardened aircraft shelters (over half of the Iraqi pre-war inventory), 113 bunkers, and 160 bridges. And all of this was accomplished flying at a rate of over twenty-six sorties per month per jet; obviously the modified and enhanced F-111Fs of Desert Storm were far more dependable than their El Dorado Canyon predecessors. But then again none of the former ever faced a fourteen-hour mission.

If the figures above are new to the reader, that is no surprise—the F-111s received very little public attention during the war. The realities of the weapons acquisition process always dictate against too much recognition for existing systems; instead, the services' public relations organizations save their silver bullets for newer machinery that requires political support for its birth and infancy. Today's F-15E, F-117 Stealth Fighter, and B-2 Stealth Bomber all fit the latter category. The crews who flew the Aardvarks in 1991 undoubtedly resented the attention lavished on the newer aircraft. But their displeasure was just an extension of what their predecessors had felt even before El Dorado Canyon.

A combination of naivete and being assigned to a "mature" (read "no political agenda attached") aircraft had led to righteous indignation among a group of 48th Wing pilots and WSOs early in 1986. They wrote to *Air Force Magazine* to express their "Aardvark Indignation" concerning a story in the periodical's January issue of that year. The article sang praises of developmental systems being procured to replace the Switchblade. The group of forty-seven(!) jet jockeys took special umbrage at a quote from an Air Force colonel suggesting that, "The F-15E is going to have the longest, lowest, toughest tactical interdiction mission in the

Air Force." They shot back that they had been doing that mission for years without various goodies installed on the Strike Eagle, and "without a word of recognition or praise from such publications as *Air Force Magazine*." They also pointed out the Aardvarks' superior speed, range, and bomb load, and ended by bragging, "We can do it today." Sent in March of 1986, the letter was published without fanfare in the May 1986 issue. They did, in fact, "do it" within days of sending the letter. Perhaps they and their Desert Storm Aardvark successors will better understand their continuing obscurity after they have read this volume.

Obviously, the wing spirit that developed in the spring of 1986 still lives on at RAF Lakenheath—the BDA from Iraq and Kuwait attests to that fact. I am certain that those who flew the Aardvark in Operation Desert Storm have a deep appreciation of the difficulties that the 1986 raid faced in comparison to their recent experience. My assessment is that their 1991 missions were flown in more dependable, modified aircraft; that they seldom exceeded four or five hours in length; that they were able to revisit targets as necessary once the Iraqi defenses were destroyed; and that those defenses were almost totally ineffective after the first few days, when Iraq's high altitude SAM capability and radar early warning systems were negated. The result was a situation described by the old saying, "shooting fish in a barrel." By saying this, I do not impugn the courage or skill of the Desert Storm flyers—they fought a smart, savvy air campaign that maximized their effectiveness and prevented a long, costly ground war. They also faced those still-intact air defenses during the first week of the air war—the Triple-A was awe inspiring no matter what your previous experience.

What the Desert Storm crews did not face was a single chance at a first-look target after a six-hour flight to the combat area. Except for the first few nights, they did not face an intact air defense system. And, perhaps most importantly, they did not then face a detailed review of their individual mission results under the microscope of worldwide publicity. Instead, each sortie's outcome, including the many that were unsuccessful for whatever reason, was lumped together into the overall, 110,000-sortie air campaign that may well be judged as history's most successful. I gladly salute the combat aviators of Desert Storm for their achievements. And I believe that they would join me in a somewhat firmer, prolonged salute as a sign of respect for the Tripoli raiders of Operation El Dorado Canyon.

The two groups of aviators also differ in one last respect. The combat crews of Desert Storm have already been publicly identified in both print and broadcast media. They wore their nametags during interviews. Some of them are undoubtedly beginning the process of documenting their experiences in books or articles; those will be published without resort to pseudonyms or to the use of initials to hide identities. Insulated against fear of reprisals by the size and scope of the war against Iraq, they feel no great concern for themselves or their families as a result of their actions in combat.

Meanwhile, the pilots and WSOs who bombed Tripoli in 1986 remain almost totally anonymous. Many of them have no wish for that status to change no matter what official U.S. government policy might be. They recognize that the unique nature of their brief combat experience may never allow them, as a group or as individuals, to publicly claim their place in aviation history. Perhaps some would consider them to be overly cautious, but there is evidence to suggest that they are merely being prudent. Over two years after the raid, eight people associated with the People's Committee for Libyan Students, including four Libyans, were arrested in the U.S. and charged with plotting assassinations of high government officials. Reports at the time were that one of the eight had supplied Tripoli with a list of U.S. government people who might have been involved in the 1986 bombing. The federal prosecutor speculated that the list was supplied for "the purpose of Libya's exacting retaliation."[5] It is not surprising that the crews who flew the mission are disinclined to take at face value the sounds of moderation now emanating from Qaddafi's Libya. They will need much more solid evidence that the threat has been removed before they give up their current anonymity.

The Air Force portion of Operation El Dorado Canyon—the first major mission in the war against terrorism, flown under truly unique circumstances and judged a significant success—may continue to be the accomplishment of a band of gallant aviators who will remain unsung for many years. Unlike their Desert Storm counterparts or even the Doolittle Raiders to whom they have been compared, they will probably not be organizing any mission-related reunions in the near future. Nevertheless, those Statue of Liberty Wing pilots and WSOs who flew the raid can take comfort in the fact that they seem to have changed the world slightly for the better that spring night in 1986.

# EPILOGUE

■

On Monday, January 16, 1989, Joyce and I drove from our home west of Baltimore to Dover AFB in Delaware to participate in the arrival ceremonies for the body of Maj. Fernando Ribas-Dominicci. After a tense, confusing weekend of mixed signals from the Libyans, one of our missing crewmen was finally coming home. But as we crossed the flat expanse of Maryland's eastern shore, many unanswered questions still remained.

There was still some doubt in my mind as to which crewman was coming home. What had really caused his death? Who besides us would be there to salute his return? The confusion regarding the first two questions had begun when the Libyans, for whatever reason, had announced that they would be turning over the body of one of the downed F-111 crewmen to the Vatican in Rome. For some reason, that announcement erroneously identified the body as that of Capt. Paul Lorence, Fernando's WSO. The mistake was not discovered until the body reached Rome where the Vatican placed it in the custody of U.S. embassy and military officials. In the meantime, Paul's family in both England and the United States had undoubtedly been notified and had probably begun to make arrangements for appropriate ceremonies and burial. By Saturday, January 14, the error had been discovered by U.S. military forensic experts, and the two families involved did their best as they struggled with their emotions. Fernando's family insisted that the body undergo an autopsy, both to confirm the identification and to pinpoint the cause of death. At this juncture anything seemed possible in light of Libya's callous actions: Colonel Qaddafi had held Fernando's body as a political bargaining chip for over two years, had only surrendered it under some duress, and finally had misidentified him into the bargain. An autopsy could at least dispel misgivings as to whether the crew had been captured alive, while also ensuring that the identification process had been correct. The family of Major Ribas-Dominicci had to know, and an autopsy seemed to be the only certain answer. The body was flown to Torrejon airbase near Madrid, Spain, where the examination was completed on Sunday, January 15.

Fernando's family received a private briefing on the post mortem after the Monday arrival ceremonies. The autopsy results were authoritative and unambiguous. They were also startling. The body was definitely that of Fernando. The cause of death was drowning. The body showed no evidence of internal injuries or fractures. The assumptions that many had made for almost three years about the cause of the F-111's downing and how its crew had died were suddenly brought into question. The Ribas-Dominicci family could take heart in knowing that the theory that the pilot of "Karma-52" had made a fatal mistake would no longer be so popular.

Through the weekend, the Air Force community in the Washington, D.C., area had gathered itself to assure that the homecoming would be well supported. Knowing that the family members were living in Texas and Puerto Rico, no one was certain that they would be able to reach Delaware on such short notice. But those of us who had been involved with the mission knew that we had to be there; to salute our fellow airman and to support his family and friends. I phoned Sam Westbrook, whose promotion to major general had just been announced, and found that he would be unable to reach Dover on the sixteenth. Instead, he was planning to attend the interment ceremonies wherever they might be once the family decided on the final arrangements. We both agreed that I ought to be in Delaware on Monday if at all possible.

On arrival at Dover, Joyce and I were steered to the chapel by base personnel well practiced in the handling of U.S. casualties from Europe and the Middle East. There we found Fernando's friends and family gathered. Despite the minimal notice, Fernando's widow and son had flown in from Texas with Air Force assistance, as had his two brothers from Puerto Rico. Almost two dozen others, mainly F-111 pilots and WSOs formerly of the 48th Wing and now serving in the Pentagon, had also come to honor their comrade. We spent a quiet hour together waiting for the inbound C-141. The time allowed each of us an appropriate channel for our emotions. We also learned of the imminent release of the autopsy's results; the family had postponed any decision on burial arrangements until after the briefing. Waiting patiently at the Dover AFB chapel, the Ribas-Dominicci family was still caught in a hellish limbo of uncertainty. They drove to the flight line in bright sunlight on a very crisp January day, praying to be released from that state.

The "humanitarian actions" of Muammar Qaddafi had put them there. The pilot's body had not proven to be useful in his attempts to unfreeze Libyan assets in the U.S. and elsewhere. Faced with hints of renewed U.S. military action against his recently identified chemical warfare capabilities, he had expediently changed his long-term stance and released it as a pacifying gesture. And then, for some unexplained reason, a mistaken identification had been made. Weeks later, in an interview with Barbara Walters, Qaddafi seemed to display his true feelings when he denied any knowledge of the whereabouts of Paul Lorence's body. He smilingly suggested that it could be found only by "the fishes." Those of us who knew Paul and sympathize with his loved ones hope that the Libyan leader was, for once, telling the truth.

The brief homecoming ceremony was conducted in silence, while the distant television cameras of the major networks recorded the event for their evening newscasts. Standing next to Fernandito, Fernando's young son, I worried that his Texan outerwear was inadequate to the stiff January breeze; he had grown out of his British woolens in the thirty-two months since his father's final mission. His mother's arm helped ward off the cold and reassured the boy, as his father's flag-draped coffin was rolled into the waiting white hearse. Blanca Ribas-Dominicci still had one last wrenching goodbye to go through, but her obvious strength and determination would undoubtedly sustain her. I held Joyce's arm tightly, blinking hard into the bright sun and stinging wind, trying not to get caught up in the blizzard of emotions that accompany the premature death of a friend. It should have been easy after over twenty years of practice—as many of my buddies had found out, longevity is not offered in the benefits package that Uncle Sam provides to fighter aircrews. But it was not easy. It was damned hard.

# NOTES

■

1. In 1991, an officer who flew on the raid took part in a television documentary on the F-111 which dealt with the mission and his role in it. Nevertheless, he is not named in this volume.
2. Documented by the Office of Air Force History, Headquarters United States Air Force, letter dated March 30, 1988.
3. Some U.S.-based tanker crews, both active and reserve, were not alerted until the afternoon of April 12. Even then, they flew nonstop to England without any idea of the mission they would be supporting, arriving Sunday afternoon with less than thirty hours remaining before the raid's takeoff. Four hours later they received their first briefing on the raid, tried to get some rest, and then began their final briefings during which all the last-minute changes had to be absorbed. Details of the tankers' story were provided in correspondence from a tanker pilot based in Louisiana who will remain anonymous in this book.

1. The colorful language of aviation often delves into black humor when describing the hazards of the trade. "Buying the farm" means dying in some farmer's field. A "granite overcast" is the worst "weather" you can fly into—solid rock. The results are always fatal.

2. The F-111 is known to have been largely the idea of ex-Secretary of Defense Robert McNamara. With the defense budget's bottom line firmly in mind, he directed a joint Navy–Air Force acquisition of the plane, insisting that it could fulfill both services' diverse missions. That plan for the F-111 was eventually abandoned.

3. Pave Tack is not an acronym. Instead, it is a system nickname assigned to the project early in its acquisition cycle by the Air Force. The arcane process that develops and assigns such nicknames is beyond the scope of this volume.

### CHAPTER TWO

1. Andrew Cockburn, "Sixty Seconds Over Tripoli," *Playboy*, May 1987, p. 132.

2. Known as a "LOADEO," such events are held periodically to test the skills and build the morale of the men and women who do one of the Air Force's most dangerous and thankless jobs. Storing, maintaining, and loading the bombs, missiles, and bullets that the combat crews deliver is not a romantic occupation. LOADEOs remind those who do it that their critical job is appreciated.

3. In wartime, keeping an airfield open for business is *the* most important task for the ninety-eight percent of the wing that is not actively flying airplanes. Identifying alternate takeoff and landing surfaces is planned well in advance, and units are prepared to operate with sharply reduced safety margins. Counting taxiways and normally closed runways, RAF Lakenheath had nearly a dozen "combat runways" available.

### CHAPTER FOUR

1. This story about the "Bloody 100th" is used as an example here due to the author's long association with that unit. An uncle served as a gunner in the group's initial cadre, and was killed in action on the Regensburg mission of August 17, 1943.

1. The author's descriptions of the 1985 terrorist actions are drawn from multiple contemporary newspaper and periodical accounts. In the case of the bombing of the La Belle Disco in Berlin, other sources dating as late as 1990 have been examined. Most have addressed the question of the validity of the U.S. information which was used to prove Libyan involvement in that attack.
2. See above.

1. Most cockpit accounts throughout this volume are drawn directly from personal written or verbal interviews with individual F-111F crewmen who flew the mission. In those cases, an attempt has been made to give their true accounts with minimal embellishment or explanatory additions. In the case of Lieutenant Colonel F. described here, the account is drawn primarily from the sources indicated below. It should be noted that the article in *Popular Mechanics* purports to be a first-hand account written by the pilot himself. However, the officer involved denies authorship. He was interviewed at length, but did not write the story. Someday Lieutenant Colonel F. will write a first-person account of his crucial role in the mission. His book will help clarify the story that I have attempted to tell here.
David Martin and John Walcott, *Best Laid Plans*. New York: Harper & Row, 1988, pp. 302–311.
A U.S. Air Force Combat Pilot, "How I Bombed Qaddafi," *Popular Mechanics*, July 1987, pp. 111–114, 153.
2. Mark Thompson, "Mixed Signals May Have Misguided U.S. Weapons," *Washington Post*, January 22, 1989, p. A4.
3. Ibid.
4. "In the Dead of the Night," *Time*, April 28, 1986, p. 20.
5. This incident has been related by several sources, all with different details as to how it was resolved. One account (from an officer then serving as the Assistant Officer in Charge of the 48th Wing's Maintenance Operations Center) indicates

that the offending person was ordered, in a fierce whisper, to keep quiet and not worry about the matter. Others relate the story as told here.

6. This story, once thought to be apocryphal, was confirmed in interviews with the chief of the wing's security police in 1986, Lt. Col. Frank Willingham, USAF.

### CHAPTER SEVEN

1. This story is one of several repeated in this volume that may be apocryphal. It is included because it has been traced to more than one second-hand source, although no first-hand account is available as of this writing.
2. As quoted in a Department of Defense Public Affairs message identified by the date/time group 150518Z APR 86.
3. The U.S. Armed Forces Network (AFN) of television and radio stations does not broadcast in the United Kingdom.
4. The claim that a fifteen-month-old girl killed in the raid was Colonel Qaddafi's adopted daughter may not be true. Questions about whether a daughter had ever been adopted were raised by U.S. officials within days of the mission. Reports of a June 19, 1986, interview of Qaddafi by United Press International indicate that he never mentioned the death of his daughter; the interviewer added a comment that "an infant girl taken in by his wife reportedly was killed." ("How Libya Conned the Media," *Human Events*, July 12, 1986.) Nevertheless, there appears to be little doubt that some members of his family were injured in the attack.
5. "MP Replies on USAF Presence Fear," *East Anglian Daily Times*, April 17, 1986, pp. 1, 25.
6. "Fears of Revenge Attacks," *Newmarket Journal*, April 17, 1986, p. 1.
7. See note 5 above.
8. Karen DeYoung, "Britain Deports 12 Libyans," *Washington Post*, April 23, 1986, p. 1.
9. See note 1 above.
10. Martin and Walcott, *Best Laid Plans*, p. 296. The book's chapter on El Dorado Canyon includes several references to

Lieutenant Colonel North's involvement in the targeting and a supposed attempt on his part to ensure that Qaddafi was in the headquarters compound that night.

**CHAPTER EIGHT**

1. Gen. Charles Donnelly, Letter to the Editor, *Defense Week*, January 5, 1987, p. 2.
2. Donald E. Fink, "Laurels for 1986," *Aviation Week & Space Technology*, January 12, 1987, p. 11.
3. See note 1 above.
4. Pat Dalton, "AF Commendation Medal Awarded Most Often," *Air Force Times*, July 6, 1987, p. 19.
5. David H. Hackworth, "The Purple Heart Takes a Hit," *Washington Post*, August 12, 1990, p. C5.
6. See note 4 above.
7. On Friday, April 25, 1986, at a Greek restaurant in Kaiserslautern, Germany, I was informed by a well-connected friend on the USAFE staff that I had not been selected to command the 48th TFW. Official notification awaited me upon my return to Lakenheath the next day. My decision to retire from the service followed shortly thereafter.
8. Details of the efforts by both the Senate and the governor of Puerto Rico to change the Air Force's decision and the service's replies to same were obtained from the U.S. Air Force through the Freedom of Information Act.
9. Gerald M. Boyd, "U.S. Is Stepping Up Rebuke to Allies on World Terror," *New York Times*, April 17, 1986, pp. 1, 2.

**CHAPTER NINE**

1. Caspar W. Weinberger, *Fighting for Peace*. New York: Warner Books, 1990, p. 198.
2. Bert Kinzey, *F-111 Aardvark*. Blue Ridge Summit, PA: Tab Books, 1989, p. 63.
3. Bernard Weinraub, "U.S. Calls Libya Raid a Success; 'Choice is Theirs,' Reagan Says; Moscow Cancels Shultz Talks," *New York Times*, April 16, 1986, p. 1.

4. James Gerstenzang, "'Major Damage' Reported on All Libyan Targets," *Los Angeles Times*, April 18, 1986.
5. See note 1 above.
6. Martin and Walcott, *Best Laid Plans*, p. 309.
7. Cockburn, "Sixty Seconds Over Tripoli," *Playboy*, 1987, p. 165.
8. Eleanor Clift, "3 Advisers to Presidents Doubt Raid Effectiveness," *Los Angeles Times*, April 29, 1986, p. 1.
9. Bill Gertz, "Terrorists Know No Borders in Their 'World War III,'" *Washington Times*, April 17, 1986, p. 10.
10. "A Defensive Air Strike That Sets the Penalties for Terrorism," *Providence Journal*, April 16, 1986.
11. Peter Almond, "Libya Squeezing Propaganda to Blacken America," *Washington Times*, April 21, 1986, p. 1.
12. Richard Matthews, "Weak, Inconsequential Europe Merits Contempt," *Atlanta Journal*, April 18, 1986, p. 18.
13. Maj. Gen. Henry Mohr, USA (Ret.), "U.S. Attack on Libya May Begin End of Terrorism," *St. Louis Globe-Democrat*, April 20, 1986.
14. David Ignatius, "Bombing Gadhafi Worked," *Washington Post*, July 13, 1986, p. B5.
    There were multiple other media reports in this vein. This article is a representative example.
15. Marcia Kunstel, "Khadafy's Tent Nearly Intact Amid the Ruins," *Dallas Morning News*, April 17, 1986, p. 1.
16. See note 14 above.
17. George Lardner Jr., "Terrorist Incidents Down 15%, State Dept. Says," *Washington Post*, May 1, 1991, p. A22.
18. See note 14 above.
19. George Lardner Jr., "French Link Libyans to Bombings," *Washington Post*, June 27, 1991, p. 1.
20. Martin and Walcott, *Best Laid Plans*, p. 290.

**CHAPTER TEN**

1. William B. Scott, "USAF Developing Better Camouflage to Protect Bases From Enemy Attack," *Aviation Week & Space Technology*, September 25, 1989, p. 85.

2. Interview with Col. Ed Dunivant, USAF (Ret.), January 16, 1990.

3. Ibid.

4. As related in written and verbal interviews with at least two El Dorado Canyon aircrew members who were still serving at Lakenheath in 1987.

5. "8 Seized for Pro-Libya Activities; One Linked to Assassination Plot," *Baltimore Sun*, July 21, 1988, p. 15.

# GLOSSARY

■

AAA: Anti-Aircraft Artillery (*see* TRIPLE-A and FLAK).

AARDVARK: Primary unofficial nickname for the F-111.

A-1E: Douglas Skyraider—a propeller-driven attack aircraft flown in Southeast Asia.

A-6: Grumman Intruder—twin-jet Navy attack aircraft.

A-7: LTV Corsair II—single-engine Navy attack aircraft.

A-10: Fairchild Republic Thunderbolt II—twin-engine Air Force attack aircraft.

AFB: Air Force Base.

AFN: Armed Forces Network—radio and television system providing service to the U.S. military overseas.

ALARM: British-designed Anti-Radiation Missile (ARM)—in development status in 1986; now operational.

ARM: Anti-Radiation Missile—a missile designed to seek and destroy radars by homing on the Radio Frequency energy they emit.

AWACS: Airborne Warning and Control System—Boeing E-3 Sentry (a 707-type airframe modified with a large radar used for early warning).

B-2: Northrop Stealth Bomber.

BINGO: Standard radio call to identify a situation where an aircraft has reached a minimum, almost-critical fuel state—in aviation slang, a descriptive term for being out of almost anything.

CALL SIGN: A name and number used in radio communications to identify a particular aircraft to friendly forces. An example from the mission is "Remit-31."

CAP: Combat Air Patrol—fighter air-to-air mission flown to find and destroy enemy aircraft.

CC: Letter designation for an Air Force unit's commander (Squadron CC; Wing CC; etc.).

CINCEUR: Commander in Chief Europe.

CINCUSAFE: Commander in Chief U.S. Air Forces in Europe.

COMM: Communications equipment.

COMM OUT: Communications equipment outage or intentional nonuse.

CND: Campaign for Nuclear Disarmament—British political movement with self-explanatory name.

CONUS: Continental United States.

CROTALE: French-built Surface-to-Air Missile (SAM).

CV: Letter designation for an Air Force unit's second in command.

DASH ONE: Crew manual for a specific aircraft—named for the suffix used to indicate its use (F-111F-*1* Manual).

DO: Like CC, a letter designation for an Air Force unit's Director of Operations or Deputy Chief of Staff for Operations.

EA-6B: Grumman Prowler—a specialized Navy Electronic Warfare aircraft.

ECM: Electronic CounterMeasures.

ECW: Electronic Combat Wing.

EF-111A: General Dynamics/Grumman Raven—a specialized Air Force Electronic Warfare aircraft (*see* SPARKVARK).

EL DORADO CANYON: Code name for the entire U.S. attack on Libya of April 14–15, 1986.

ELECTRIC JET: Unofficial nickname for General Dynamics F-16.

EUCOM: European Command headquartered at Stuttgart, Germany (*see* USEUCOM), joint headquarters for all U.S. forces in Europe.

EW: Electronic Warfare.

EWO: Electronic Warfare Officer.

F-4: McDonnell Douglas Phantom fighter aircraft used by both the Air Force and the Navy.

F-4G: Phantom modified for electronic warfare and defense suppression (also known as Wild Weasel).

F-14: Grumman Tomcat Navy fighter aircraft for air-to-air mission.

F-15: McDonnell Douglas Eagle Air Force fighter aircraft—primarily air-to-air.

F-15E: F-15 modified for air-to-ground missions (also known as the Strike Eagle).

F-16: General Dynamics Fighting Falcon Air Force multirole fighter aircraft.

F-100: North American Super Sabre Air Force fighter aircraft.

F-105: Republic Thunderchief Air Force fighter aircraft (*see* THUD).

F-111: General Dynamics Air Force fighter aircraft for air-to-ground mission (*see* AARDVARK and SWITCHBLADE).

F-111F: The latest variant of the F-111, flown operationally only by the 48th Tactical Fighter Wing.

F-117A: Lockheed Stealth Fighter Air Force aircraft.

F/A-18: McDonnell Douglas Hornet multirole Navy fighter aircraft.

FEET WET: Radio call used to indicate that an aircraft has crossed the coast outbound to sea.

FIGHTER JOCK: Slang for "fighter jockey"—anyone who flies or crews a fighter or attack aircraft.

FLAK: Anti-Aircraft Artillery (*see* AAA and TRIPLE-A).

FLOGGER: Soviet swing-wing fighter-bomber (also known as MiG-23).

GBU-10: Designation for a type of 2,000-pound Laser Guided Bomb.

GBU-12: Designation for a type of 500-pound Laser Guided Bomb.

GMT: Greenwich Mean Time—the world's baseline time based on the British meridian; Libyan time is GMT plus two hours.

GORILLA: Fighter pilot slang for a huge aerial armada; the El Dorado Canyon Air Force task force was an example.

HARM: Texas Instruments High-speed Anti-Radiation Missile—the primary defense suppression munition of the U.S.

HAS: Hardened Aircraft Shelter—bomb-resistant concrete-and-steel shelter used to protect aircraft (*see* TAB Vee).

HF: High Frequency.

IFF: Identification Friend or Foe—electronic system used to distinguish between friendly aircraft and enemy and allow attack of the latter without fratricide.

INS: Inertial Navigation System—primary self-contained, gyroscopic navigation system carried on U.S. aircraft.

IP: Initial Point—last turn or check point prior to target.

KC-10: McDonnell Douglas Extender—modified DC-10 aircraft used as aerial refueling tanker.

KC-135: Boeing Stratotanker—modified B-707 aircraft used as aerial refueling tanker.

KIA: Killed In Action.

LGB: Laser Guided Bomb.

LOM: Legion Of Merit medal.

MARK 82: A 500-pound unguided bomb.

MARK 84: A 2,000-pound unguided bomb.

MED: Slang name for Mediterranean Sea.

MIA: Missing In Action.

MiG: A type of Soviet fighter aircraft (also used as a generic term for all Russian fighters).

MSM: Meritorious Service Medal.

NAF: Numbered Air Force (i.e. Third Air Force at Mildenhall).

NATO: North Atlantic Treaty Organization.

NCO: Non-Commissioned Officer.

PAVE TACK: An infrared and laser targeting system installed in the F-111F.

PRAIRIE FIRE: Code name for the U.S. Navy Freedom of Navigation operations near Libya—March 22–26, 1986.

PRIME PUMP: Initial code name for the operation that was later executed as Operation El Dorado Canyon.

PUC: Presidential Unit Citation.

RAF: Royal Air Force.

ROE: Rules Of Engagement.

SA-: Designation of hostile SAMs, with the number indicating the particular missile (SA-2, SA-3, etc.).

SAC: Strategic Air Command.

SAM: Surface-to-Air Missile.

SPARKVARK: Unofficial nickname for the EF-111 Raven.

SPECAT: Special Category.

SWITCHBLADE: Another unofficial nickname for the F-111.

TAB Vee: An aircraft shelter (*see* HAS), named for "Theater Air Base Vulnerability" shelter.

TAC: Tactical Air Command.

TACAN: Tactical Air Navigation—a navigation system that locates aircraft in relation to surface-based electronic beacons.

TF: Terrain-Following.

TFS: Tactical Fighter Squadron.

TFW: Tactical Fighter Wing.

THUD: Unofficial nickname for the F-105 Thunderchief.

TLAR: That Looks About Right—pilots' term for a dependable low-tech way of judging things in the air.

TORNADO: European strike aircraft flown by several NATO countries including Great Britain, Germany, and Italy.

TOT: Time Over Target or Time On Target.

TRIPLE-A: Anti-Aircraft Artillery (*see* AAA or FLAK).

USAF: United States Air Force.

USAFE: United States Air Forces in Europe.

USEUCOM: United States European Command (*see* EUCOM).

WSO: Weapons Systems Operator or Weapons System Officer—in an F-111, the right-seater whose duties go well beyond the descriptive name.

# INDEX

■

## ABOUT THE AUTHOR

■

As the Vice Wing Commander of the 48th TFW, Col. Robert E. Venkus played a major role in planning and executing the April 14–15, 1986, raid on Tripoli, Libya. During over twenty-four years in the U.S. Air Force, he logged over 4,000 flying hours in a variety of trainers and fighters, including almost 1,200 hours and 169 combat missions in the F-105. His numerous awards include the Legion of Merit, the Distinguished Flying Cross with one Oak Leaf Cluster, and the Air Medal with thirteen Oak Leaf Clusters. His assignments included tours as a fighter squadron commander and as the staff director in charge of all USAF fighter operations and training in Europe. Colonel Venkus retired from the Air Force in 1987 and is now employed as a manager in the defense electronics industry. He and his wife Joyce reside in Ellicott City, Maryland.